AF756876

'*Applying the Person-Centred Approach to Global, Social and Personal Crises* is a timely and much-needed book. It explores how Carl Rogers' principles empower individuals and communities to navigate social upheavals and trauma with empathy and authenticity, bridging personal healing and global transformation. Read and relish it!'

Peggy Natiello, PhD, *International Consultant on Client-Centred Therapy and the PCA, USA*

'This is person-centred practice at its most exciting and innovative: creative and resourceful in the most hostile of environments. It is inspirational to see the power of this relational approach to facilitate connection, healing and hope in different contemporary situations and to read the passion, commitment and activism of practitioners.'

Suzanne Keys, *Supervisor and School and College Counsellor, UK*

Applying the Person-Centred Approach to Global, Social and Personal Crises

Against the backdrop of current debates in society about mental health and responses to crises, this edited volume examines the person-centred approach (PCA) as a vital framework for addressing contemporary mental health challenges and promoting psychosocial resilience across diverse cultural contexts.

This book tackles a range of themes and topics that reflect challenging, contemporary global, social, and personal issues, such as war and conflict, social care, grief and loss, artificial intelligence, and neurodiversity. Chapters explore the universal issues that face the person-centred, experiential, and humanistic counselling communities in our current times, as well as the barriers to addressing these issues, and the models of good, innovative practice that have sought to tackle them. This book demonstrates how non-directivity proves to be crucial for affecting meaningful change for the self. Presenting first-hand practitioner experience and guidance, this book will be of significant value amidst current dialogue and debate on the value of the PCA when working with people and organisations in times of crises.

Focusing on the wider application of the PCA beyond the therapy room and the response it offers to current societal challenges, this book will be essential reading for person-centred practitioners, counselling researchers and policymakers interested in crises, conflicts, and social changes.

Mairi McMenamin is an independent Person-Centred Counsellor, Supervisor and Trainer, UK.

Kate Munro is an independent consultant in Person-Centred Education, UK.

Explorations in Mental Health

Mental Healthcare in Brazilian Spiritism: The Aesthetics of Healing
Helmar Kurz

Exploring Creative Wellbeing Frameworks in Context
Nature, Culture, and Sustainable Futures
Edited by Wenche Torrissen and Helga S. Løvoll

A Transdisciplinary Study of Addiction
A New Framework for Drug Policy Reform
Francisco Blancarte Jaber

A Creative Health Communication Framework
Addressing the Compatibility and Marketability of Mental Health and Wellbeing Services
Jane Hearst

Afro-Caribbean Dynamics of Sexuality and Relationships
Reclaiming the Caribbean Sexual Narrative
Kai A. D. Morgan Campbell

Applying the Person-Centred Approach to Global, Social and Personal Crises
Contemporary Challenges
Edited by Mairi McMenamin and Kate Munro

For more information about this series, please visit www.routledge.com/Explorations-in-Mental-Health/book-series/EXMH

Applying the Person-Centred Approach to Global, Social and Personal Crises

Contemporary Challenges

Edited by
Mairi McMenamin and Kate Munro

Routledge
Taylor & Francis Group
LONDON AND NEW YORK

First published 2026
by Routledge
4 Park Square, Milton Park, Abingdon, Oxon OX14 4RN

and by Routledge
605 Third Avenue, New York, NY 10158

Routledge is an imprint of the Taylor & Francis Group, an informa business

© 2026 selection and editorial matter, Mairi McMenamin and Kate Munro; individual chapters, the contributors

The right of Mairi McMenamin and Kate Munro to be identified as the authors of the editorial material, and of the authors for their individual chapters, has been asserted in accordance with sections 77 and 78 of the Copyright, Designs and Patents Act 1988.

All rights reserved. No part of this book may be reprinted or reproduced or utilised in any form or by any electronic, mechanical, or other means, now known or hereafter invented, including photocopying and recording, or in any information storage or retrieval system, without permission in writing from the publishers.

Trademark notice: Product or corporate names may be trademarks or registered trademarks, and are used only for identification and explanation without intent to infringe.

British Library Cataloguing-in-Publication Data
A catalogue record for this book is available from the British Library

ISBN: 978-1-032-87128-8 (hbk)
ISBN: 978-1-032-88055-6 (pbk)
ISBN: 978-1-003-53604-8 (ebk)

DOI: 10.4324/9781003536048

Typeset in Times New Roman
by codeMantra

This book is for Angela, who taught us how to live a life that is unconditional, and for Agnes, whose constant encouragement, love and support made it possible.

Contents

About the Editors

Mairi McMenamin worked in nursing, midwifery, social science and public health before qualifying as a person-centred counsellor with a post-graduate diploma from the University of Strathclyde. She is also a person-centred supervisor with a diploma in person-centred supervision and for many years worked in a board capacity for PCE World and in the Co-ordinating Group of PCT Scotland. Although she had spent her early career in the helping professions, her first encounter with the PCA was transformative, like finding herself 'at home'. Since then, she has worked as a counsellor, a supervisor and a trainer with an undiminished passion for the person-centred approach.

Dr. Kate Munro has post-graduate qualifications in medicine and special education. After a career in education, disability services and health, she now works as an independent consultant in person-centred education, a writer and is an Associate Editor of the *Journal of the Royal Asiatic Society, China*.

Contributors

Terry Daly is a person-centred counsellor, supervisor and educator. He works in health, social work, the private and voluntary sectors, and within university settings. Terry's private practice focuses on helping individuals and organisations live and work more effectively. He offers individual therapeutic support, emotional coaching, psychological support and mentoring, and assists organisations with policy and procedures. Terry is committed to the development of the person-centred approach, has written a number of papers and for PCCS books and has held committee positions, both within PCT Scotland and European networks.

Elektra Diakolambrianou is a person-centred psychotherapist and trainer with post-graduate studies in applied art therapies, creative writing, cinematherapy, guided imagery and music, bibliotherapy, game-based education, restorative justice and social psychology. She has long experience of working with socially vulnerable groups, including unaccompanied minors, refugees, immigrants, NEETs, victims of mass layoffs and former prisoners. She is an academic faculty member at the Institution for Counselling and Psychological Studies in Athens, Greece as well as an external associate of the Transformative Play Initiative at the Department of Game Design of Uppsala University in Sweden. She is also a co-founder of LARPifiers, a non-profit company that specialises in the use of live-action role-playing and other game-based methodologies as tools for education, personal development and psychotherapy.

Yana Gololob, MA Psychology, is a person-centred psychotherapist in private practice, a trainer and supervisor of the Ukrainian Umbrella Association of Psychotherapists, a lecturer at the Ukrainian Psychotherapy University and a guest lecturer at the Dortmund University of Applied Sciences and Arts. She is a PCE World Board Member. Her main concern is with the development of the person-centred approach, both in Ukraine and worldwide. In this regard, she has contributed to and co-edited, together with Gina Di Malta, Mick Cooper, Maureen O'Hara and Susan Stephen, *The*

Handbook of Person-Centred Psychotherapy & Counselling, 3rd edition (Bloomsbury, 2024).

Sonny Hallett is a person-centred counsellor and supervisor based in Edinburgh, Scotland. They are trans, autistic and mixed race, and these and other personal and community experiences inform a lot of their thinking and therapeutic work. They are active within autistic and disability advocacy communities, and co-founded and chaired AMASE (Autistic Mutual Aid Society Edinburgh). They also work on research, writing and training relating to difference and diversity. They are particularly interested in the ways in which counselling training, supervision and practice can reinforce normative ideas at the expense of diversity, and how we might challenge and counter that.

Stephanie Hutchinson had a career in television production before training as a person-centred counsellor and qualifying with a post-graduate diploma from the University of Strathclyde. She is also a Certified Daring Way™ facilitator. After 18 years in Scotland, she returned to her native New Zealand where she maintains a small private practice as well as providing grief counselling in the hospice setting and death literacy education within the Compassionate Communities space.

Jen Keppie worked in intensive care nursing before studying for a post-graduate diploma in person-centred counselling with Persona Development and Training. Based in the Highlands of Scotland, she works for a Scottish baby loss charity, offering counselling support to families across the region who have experienced the loss of a baby or young child. In addition, she runs her own small private practice with a particular interest in working outdoors and the intersection of the PCA with the field of eco-therapy.

Susanna Markowitsch worked as a translator and management assistant in various areas before qualifying as a person-centred psychotherapist with a diploma from APG.IPS, Austria. From her first encounter with the PCA, she was enthusiastic and passionate about the PCA, and this remains unchanged. She has, for many years, worked in various board capacities for PCE World and APG.IPS, Austria. She now works as a person-centred psychotherapist, counsellor and supervisor in private practice in Austria as well as a trainer for APG.IPS, Austria, and post-graduate psychotherapy training at the University of Vienna.

Gareth Pierce is a qualified person-centred counsellor and Professor of Electrical & Electronic Engineering at the University of Strathclyde, Glasgow, Scotland. His interests include understanding the impact of machine learning and AI technologies on the counselling and psychotherapy professions.

Jacquelyn Pratt is an independent practitioner in private practice in Glasgow, UK. After gaining her post-graduate diploma from the University of Strathclyde, she worked in Addictions before finding her vocation specialising in Relationship Therapy.

Alex Vallidis is a psychologist and person-centred psychotherapist (BSc, MSc, ECP) based in Athens, Greece. He serves as Academic Lead at ICPS College for Humanistic Sciences, where he trains and supervises students in psychotherapy. His clinical and research interests focus on relational trauma, grief and refugee mental health. Since 2023, he has been a researcher with UNHCR–PRAKSIS, exploring person-centred approaches to trauma in displaced children. He also founded 'Anikein/Belonging', a centre supporting student development and reflective practice. Alex is the author of *Person-Centred and Experiential Counseling for relational trauma* (PCE-rt) and holds leadership roles in PCE Europe, PCE World, and the European Association for Psychotherapy.

Foreword

It is my privilege to have known Mairi McMenamin, one of the editors of this book, for almost seven years. We first met in Vienna in 2018 at the conference of the World Association of Person-Centred and Experiential Psychotherapy and Counselling, PCE2018, when Mairi was a board member. This event, with its theme of 'hope', celebrated the approach in its wealth, relevance and availability. For me, it was the first international, professional event I ever attended abroad, and I appreciated Mairi's attitude, which was both welcoming and very accepting in embracing all my curiosity about the role of the association in settling the approach around the world.

A lot of water has flowed under the bridge since then, and the world has changed, becoming a place where fewer and fewer people are offered a safe space; crises such as pandemics and wars have had a significant impact. Therapists and counsellors are now faced with the challenge of supporting clients with overly complex processes while being of help not only in a therapeutic way, but also in disseminating these principles beyond the framework of their practice. These new challenges, which are encountered on personal, social and even global levels, require deep knowledge and experience from the professionals in the field.

It takes much existential courage to engage with the global challenges of war, conflict, asylum seeking, etc.; to face up to the social issues that threaten our collective sense of safety and certainty; to facilitate a process for those that experience trauma and profound loss and the courage to resist offering remedies, easy solutions or quick fixes. Most of us are confident that the person-centred approach provides the space and conditions under which a person can be encountered in an empathic, authentic and non-judgemental way, being empowered with an integration of sense of self and the new capacities that profoundly enhance the journey of their lives, no matter how difficult it may be at that moment. Being a Ukrainian PCA therapist, I learnt that the approach can also be applicable in different contexts, even when both the therapist and client are working under circumstances where the clients' existential experiences evoke existential experiences and even shattering in therapists. In times of war, these experiences, as a shared crisis, can overlap more than ever.

I believe that this book may be profoundly helpful for a wide range of readers, including anyone who is curious about the approach, and not just for the further development of specialists in the field. Indeed, it is a splendid source of knowledge about how the PCA can nowadays be relevant, not only for providing personal growth but also in addressing broader issues in the social and political landscape. This book showcases a collection of remarkable stories from many parts of the world, told in different voices and highlighting diverse perspectives on the application of the PCA. At the same time, the reader can find it interesting and perhaps even surprising how the principles and values introduced by Carl Rogers more than 70 years ago can still be beneficial when planted in the relational soil that is fertilised by non-directive attitude, an atmosphere of the necessary and sufficient conditions and a commitment by professionals to take into account all the personal, cultural and local indigenous aspects.

I admire the desire of the editors and all the contributors to the book to show that the PCA still remains a radical approach, sufficient for a wide range of current challenges, not rigid but evolving and alive. The argument for this is the common traits that can be found in all of these narratives, which demonstrate the power of growth and transformation.

Yana Gololob
Dnipro, Ukraine, 2025
PCA Therapist
PCE World Board Member

Introduction

In this book, we want to celebrate the person-centred approach (PCA) and to demonstrate its power in contemporary global, social and personal crises. It presents a seemingly eclectic collection of stories from person-centred practice, but we see a common thread in these stories. They each demonstrate the value and applicability of the PCA as they explore the challenging, universal issues facing the person-centred and experiential counselling community at this time. The authors identify the barriers to addressing these issues and the power of the practice that has emerged to tackle them, and, in doing so, they not only demonstrate unequivocally that the PCA is powerful and effective but also reaffirm its universal value.

This book not only acknowledges the work of Carl Rogers, the father of the PCA, but also pays tribute to our colleague Peter F. Schmid, sadly missed, whose wisdom and reflections on philosophical, sociological and psychological perspectives within the PCA continue to add enormous value to the person-centred community.

When the PCA emerged in the 1950s from the work of Carl Rogers, it was a radical approach to helping people. Rogers' early focus in his psychotherapy practice was on facilitating growth but he moved from what he originally called client-centred therapy to expand his theory on human development to the PCA. In this, the principal factor is the development of relationship, one with another; it is radical because it is a way of letting go of power and a move away from mechanistic approaches to one of growth-facilitation.

In Rogers' book *A Way of Being*,[1] he articulates the approach as a way of being in the world. It is not a tool, not a technique, but a central belief and commitment to be authentic in ones' life and in wider society; to be relational in working with others. This includes striving to be unconditional, accepting of difference in others and is an intrinsically active way of being. Rogers' thesis was that if the therapist can provide a growth-producing psychological climate, then the person moves to greater self-understanding and hopefully towards more life-giving ways of being in the world. He described six necessary and sufficient conditions, of which there are three core attitudes or conditions, that the therapist needs to provide for the client, the group or the

DOI: 10.4324/9781003536048-1

social system. The core conditions are congruence, empathy and unconditional positive regard, described by Natiello[2] as a trinity; inseparable, mutual and interdependent.

These necessary and sufficient conditions, laid out by Rogers more than 70 years ago, defined and continue to define the PCA. We believe the PCA remains relevant to global, social and individual challenges because, at its core, it is democratic, respectful of human frailty, non-directive and accepting.

However, in recent dialogue, both in and beyond the person-centred community, there has been renewed reflection on and sometimes dismissal of the PCA. Whilst not new, this debate currently feels like it is increasing in volume. The misunderstandings about the true meaning of the approach include it being seen as needing to change, not applicable to trauma or no longer relevant. We believe that these perspectives misrepresent the PCA. In this book, we showcase practitioners with a real understanding of the depth and value of the approach; those whose everyday practice demonstrates that the PCA is well suited to the global, social and personal crises that confront us. Their descriptions of offering the core conditions in a humanistic, non-directive way confirm the effectiveness of the approach and demonstrate that being heard and accepted for who we are matters, however great the challenge.

Many of the authors in this book come from personal and professional connections made through conferences and meetings with colleagues from Scotland, Europe and the wider world, with whom we share a deep understanding of the value of the PCA. Each was invited to tell their own story, to talk about their practice and how they apply the PCA. Some authors who work in a European context use the terminology PCE, person-centred and experiential approach but, while there may be slight differences in their language, their application of the approach is the same. In each chapter, you will hear the authors' and their clients' distinctive voices as they describe how offering the conditions of the PCA enables change and growth, whether that is in the therapy room or in education, health, social care or other organisations.

There are many challenges leading to distress in our society. We outline below the ones that are discussed in this book; some are global, some social and some deeply personal but all have been transformed by the power of the PCA.

Section 1: Global Challenges, Global Issues

The first section examines the role of the PCA in tackling some of the major global challenges and conflicts in the world today. These chapters show the deep and enduring value of the PCA, describing the barriers faced and the effective responses developed by person-centred practitioners.

In Chapter 1, Susanna Markowitsch reflects on global challenges and the value of the application of the PCA. She documents how, with a person-centred attitude, we can facilitate change and development in global crises and recognise the accompanying development at both an individual and a wider level.

In Chapter 2, Alex Vallidis and Elektra Diakolambrianou introduce us to their work with refugees, asylum seekers and unaccompanied children in Greece, identifying the barriers faced when those working from a relational and non-directive approach are engaged in complex, demanding, global scenarios. They describe how burnout, workload and bureaucracy can impact the practitioner and propose solutions that enhance emotional resilience and help sustain compassionate care.

Finally, in this section, Chapter 3 describes Mairi and Terry Daly's experience of working with Ukrainian therapists in a time of war. Working across modalities, with people in severe trauma and with significant differences in culture, understanding and language, they nevertheless show how empathy, congruence, unconditional positive regard and non-directivity provided a safe, nourishing space that strengthened these therapists and allowed them to continue to support their clients.

Section 2: The PCA and Social Change

In Section 2, we look at how the PCA is responding to emerging social pressures and its application in areas that are in some ways 'new'. We see how the PCA has powerful applications both inside and outside the therapy room.

First, in this section, Chapter 4 by Kate and Terry Daly showcases the application of the PCA in response to a recruitment crisis in social care. While perhaps not an obvious approach to recruitment, this chapter describes how the application of the PCA provided positive outcomes for employers, staff and clients alike.

In Chapter 5, Gareth Pierce tackles artificial intelligence (AI), technology and the PCA. He outlines the rapid growth of AI and reflects on its potential impact on counselling in the future. Gareth challenges us to be open to the benefits and applications of AI, especially in the light of the increasing demands being placed on mental health services, and presents some challenging questions for readers to ponder.

Chapter 6, by Sonny Hallett, explores the growing awareness of neurodiversity, its presentation in the therapy room and the lessons it has for person-centred practice. There are many parallels between the PCA and ways of being in community that have organically emerged in marginalised and minoritised communities, like those who describe themselves as neurodiverse. Sonny explores these parallels and asks questions of practitioners by way of processing their own reflections on self, others and difference, making links with queer, trans and mixed race spaces.

Section 3: The PCA in Universal Issues and Personal Trauma

The final section focuses on universal issues of personal crisis, issues that challenge and discomfit us. These chapters show the PCA to be a nurturing, growthful approach, even in the most challenging of scenarios.

Chapter 7 highlights the value of the PCA in working with ex-convicts. Facilitating the return is how the author, Elektra Diakolambrianou, frames her work. Like social care, our justice systems also find themselves under great pressure, seeking solutions to problems of overcrowding, breakdown of trust in the established systems and recidivism. In response, Elektra describes the PCA as an effective approach, presenting insights on offender-based counselling, the transient nature of the work and a deep valuing of unconditional positive regard, congruence and the client as a whole person.

The next chapter, Chapter 8, examines the PCA and the end of life. Here Stephanie Hutchinson writes of a perspective on death and dying that reflects people living longer in the Western world and the medicalisation of death and dying whilst at the same time acknowledging a move towards the concept of compassionate communities and public health approaches to palliative care. She argues for 'no more deathly silences' and acknowledges the value of the PCA in appreciating both individual and collective experience and human relationality at the end of life.

Chapter 9 explores relationship resilience and growth as Jacquelyn Pratt introduces us to her work with couples. Relationships underpin everything we do and can be the difference between functioning in potentiality or in deficit. Jacquelyn describes how the PCA, as a collaborative process between client and therapist, creates the conditions for the growth of a relationship within a non-directive environment. She emphasises the importance of stating her core sense of her own person-centredness, a valuing of relationship and the crucial importance of congruence.

Finally, in Chapter 10, we meet Jen Keppie writing about the importance of the PCA in working with baby loss. Here she beautifully outlines the profound loss experienced by parents and the response of wider society, which includes a lack of understanding of the enormity of loss. The application of the PCA is clearly articulated as is the value of providing an unconditional space for loss to be processed.

Our grateful thanks go to our authors, who brought their passion for the PCA to this book. As editors, we appreciate their hard work, collaboration in peer review with other authors and the beautiful prose with which they have so clearly expressed their application of the PCA and the lessons from it for all practitioners. Thank you.

Thanks also to our Editorial Advisory Group, Susan Stephen and Lesley Gray, who supported, encouraged and safely guided us through the challenges in developing the book and to AnnaMary Goodall at Routledge for her ever generous advice, support and encouragement.

We hope that both existing and newly qualified practitioners will find that this book and the inspirational work of our authors provide a reconnection to their commitment to the PCA and a helpful reflection on practice.

Mairi McMenamin and Kate Munro

Notes

1 Rogers, C.R., *A Way of Being* (New York: Houghton Mifflin, 1980)
2 Natiello, P., *The Person Centred Approach: A Passionate Presence* (Monmouth: PCCS Books Limited, 2001)

Section 1

Global Challenges, Global Issues

1 The Person-Centred Approach in Global Challenge and Global Change

Susanna Markowitsch

A lot comes to mind when we start to consider today's global challenges and global change: wars and oppression, threats to democracies, pandemics, climate catastrophe – we'd rather not think further, it is too painful. When I think about the current global challenges, I often feel despondent, desperate and powerless. I ask myself what I can do personally, whether my attitude, my way of being and thinking, can be a support for myself and others, and is there anything the person-centred approach (PCA) can offer? Carl R. Rogers died almost 40 years ago and developed the PCA decades ago, in what was a very different world. Rogers' political involvement and his international work for peace come to mind, but, where are we now? Is the PCA present and helpful in today's global context?

And then I think about my psychotherapeutic and supervisory work with clients, my experience in encounter groups, with students and colleagues of psychotherapy, the moments when I am close to people affected by global challenges; people who are frightened, hopeless, physically and mentally in bad shape, in danger, confronted with hatred and not understood. What is the role and value of the PCA, are we able to give effective responses? I think we, as person-centred practitioners, do. In my practice, I have the opportunity to accompany people in their development process, where they accept personal challenges and find highly individual ways to better deal with them.

There is the young medical student who organises peace camps for kids from Israel and Palestine, offering a quiet, safe environment in the Austrian mountains to encounter and play.

There was a young woman, distressed about the world situation and the highly personal and professional challenges she faced – a partner with diametrically opposed political views, changed working conditions after the company she worked for was sold to an international corporation and the after-effects of isolation during the COVID pandemic – but, she found her own way of better dealing with these very different challenges.

And the supervisee, a nurse who was in burnout but now takes good care of herself and has made suggestions for work improvements to nursing management.

DOI: 10.4324/9781003536048-3

A Basis for Tackling Global Challenges

When I think about how I can personally deal with the current challenges and which theoretical considerations are helpful, I always rely on the following supports: on one hand Rogers' person-centred theory[1] and on the other Peter F. Schmid's assertion that the PCA can provide hope on an individual and a global level and 'Psychotherapy is Political or it is not Psychotherapy'.[2]

One of Rogers' most significant achievements was the formulation of the six necessary and, in his opinion, sufficient conditions for personality development through psychotherapy. 'No other conditions are necessary. If these six conditions exist and continue over a period of time, this is sufficient. The process of constructive personality change will follow'.[3] These six conditions read like a general description of any psychotherapy and are relevant for constructive human co-existence, in general.

The so-called core conditions, congruence, unconditional positive regard (UPR) and empathy, seem to be basic training for various psychotherapy schools and everybody in a helping profession seems to 'use' them. And this is where the PCA makes the difference! The core conditions are not preconditions, but the only conditions necessary for the helping person's attitude and their way of being. The crucial point is the relationship between helper and client, between persons; the conditions cannot be used as a therapeutic instrument, but 'relation is therapy', according to Peter F. Schmid.

Peter F. Schmid (1950–2020) was one of my most important and influential trainers in person-centred psychotherapy. I still miss our theoretical discussions and my encounters with him. Peter was not only a practical theologian and pastoral psychologist but also a person-centred psychotherapist and theorist. He was the author of numerous profound publications and articles on psychotherapy, philosophy, theology and politics. He was a committed advocate of the person-centred approach as a practice that develops its encounter-oriented commitment from a socio-ethical responsibility. Peter taught me to understand the PCA dialogically, radically and politically. This means seeing the person in their independence while, at the same time, being dependent on relationships.

What Can an Attitude Based on Empathy Achieve in a Challenging World?

Empathy, as I understand it, goes beyond the colloquial meaning of feeling with another person, but means to be open to another's reality and be touched by it. It suggests acknowledgement of diversity, similarity and difference, to try to understand the other person as if I were them without losing myself; and this implies the risk that I might change myself! Empathy can be seen as a bridge between persons, as it is not about a winner or loser, not about removing or levelling differences or gaps, but about realising the difference between persons without surrendering. In an ideal setting, this kind of relationship is experienced without judgement or interpretation. Empathy, then, is not about making things visible for the other, but is like a joint attempt to try to understand better, it is a process.

I have experienced Rogers' exemplary example of empathy[4] in counselling sessions. Sometimes my clients' reaction to what I have said reminds me to critically question whether I've empathically understood them. Rogers shows the difference between superficial understanding of the other and the person-centred meaning of empathy, with a corresponding effect on the client and on the relationship between client and counsellor,

> If I, as a counsellor, tell my client what I have superficially understood of what the client has just said, the client might say something like "Of course, this is what I have just said", This will not have an effect on the client's self-exploration. If I express a real empathic reaction, the client's reaction might be, "Yes, that's true. I never had thought that anybody could understand what I really meant. Now I would like to tell you more about it". If I succeed in understanding the subtle meanings at the edge of my client's consciousness, the first reaction of my client might be a pause, followed by a step-by-step insight, such as, "Yes, I think you are right… I haven't seen it that way before, but this is what I have felt and experienced for such a long time... now I see more clearly".

I often find it challenging to attempt to enter the inner world of another person and remain in such a relationship, encountering the other person with empathy, especially when the other person seems to reject me and my being this way in this relationship. Nevertheless, if I focus on the other person's experience, trying to follow this person wherever they move to, I am at the same time present for the other as a person. It is essential that my empathic efforts to understand are perceived by the other person, therefore it is necessary to communicate it. Thus, the fact of trying to understand allows for possible change and development; 'change through understanding'.[5]

Congruence in a Changing World

Here congruence comes into play, without which empathic attitude in the relationship cannot be understood. Being congruent does not mean to be authentic in the sense of saying whatever comes into my mind, being congruent is much more part of a way of being the person one is. This means that I'm open to any experience, but it also needs the relational aspect of communicating this to the other person. Communicating congruence means that I can only speak from my own perspectives and my inner experiences. Trusting in my own experience and being familiar with myself, will result in trustworthiness to others.

Being congruent means that I don't hide behind a façade such as that of 'expert', or pretend to be different by adapting to others or adopting a prevailing opinion: 'If the person is thoroughly congruent then it is clear that all of his communication would necessarily be put in a context of personal perception. This has very important implications'.[6] It is a 'sincere person-to-person relationship between two imperfect people'.[7]

I admit that I sometimes find it difficult to be congruent with clients, because I think that I can't bother them with my own feelings. Again and again, though, I experience that my being congruent and being genuinely myself as a person with my clients is so very helpful for our relationship and for the clients' understanding of themselves. And thereby, I avoid the temptation to hide behind my professionalism. When I tell my client that I feel saddened by what I have just heard or that I'm getting annoyed, I do not judge or mean that what I have just heard IS sad or that my client IS annoying. Clients usually experience and understand me as a person in these moments, but also a confrontation with a client who might feel judged is usually helpful for both of us and clarifies our relationship. I experience my being congruent and verbalising my feelings as always helpful for our relationship.

After having expressed my feelings, they change and I'm able to again encounter my client empathically and my client will also answer congruently in response to having experienced my being congruent; this allows for our relationship to continue. In my experience my authenticity and trying to be genuine and communicate congruence does facilitate the other's possibility of congruence in themselves. Being congruent means that I am visible as a person, which may result in attacks and criticism, but we do need 'the other' to confront us with the global and societal challenges, to empathically try to understand the other, whilst congruently remaining the person we are, and be visible as who we are. This can be quite a challenge at times!

In my experience, a fundamental attitude, based on empathy and congruence, becomes visible in relationships and may facilitate openness in others. Of course, such an attitude stands in stark contrast to the usual mainstream of expert opinions and (supposed) certainties, but this is exactly what is needed to enable communication, encounter, dialogue. It requires a self-image with a convinced attitude and the courage to show oneself.

Hope as an Agent of Change

This attitude in connection with global challenges leads me to think of hope. Schmid says that we have to differentiate between hope as the goal of hope in the future and the process of hoping as a part of humanness.[8] From a person-centred point of view, he says, hope can be seen as the 'voice' of the actualising tendency, realising itself in many ways, even when we're not aware of it: implying that hope is a resource and competence of a person.

> ...the present societal and political challenges can be met by a person-centred understanding of hope and trust: the task is not to raise hopes, but to facilitate hope; not to aim at solutions in order to change the world, but to encounter it.[9]

In the context of psychotherapy, and in the larger context, that means that the helping person facilitates hope. This facilitation is only possible through the helper's way of being with the client/other, through their presence, their congruence, UPR and empathy.

It is a logical consequence to see the PCA as a political approach, as Schmid said, 'Psychotherapy is Political or is not Psychotherapy'. 'The approach, by its very nature, is a socially critical and thus socio-political approach, a fundamental programme for a therapy of the society, a psychotherapy and sociotherapy (in the meaning of a therapy of and for society). The approach by its very nature is a programme for radical societal transformation and thus (socio-) political change'.[10]

The Political Aspect of the PCA

Politics is often reduced to the meaning of power issues, but the PCA is highly political when we encounter the other empathically and communicate congruently, as opposed to trying to control them or imposing our will. On a societal level, this means that we facilitate an awareness of the PCA and its values when we try to understand the others' views and values and at the same time communicate our own values and confront others with them. Yes, it is one thing to work with clients behind closed doors, but it is another thing to position myself publicly, engage with people outside of my practice and make myself visible.

We must remain true to our convictions and join groups of people who share our values, we need to strengthen international and national organisations, such as PCE World or PCE Europe. We know from experience that organisations do make a difference in difficult times. Whether that is by positioning themselves publicly, for example, PCE Europe with a statement on the invasion of Ukraine or other organisations offering psychotherapy pro bono for those affected by war and persecution. Organisations can help and support people in difficult situations such as PCE World acknowledging inequities in the world with its Financial Aid Resources (FAiR) fund.

Rogers proposed that the more the PCA is implemented and put into practice, the more it is found to challenge hierarchical models of 'treatment' and hierarchical methods of organisation. 'The very effectiveness of this unified person-centred approach constitutes a threat to professionals, administrators, and others, and steps are taken – consciously and unconsciously – to destroy it. It is too revolutionary'.[11] The PCA is still revolutionary and opposed to present political ideas, but I don't think that this approach is too revolutionary, I think it is still too quiet.

Criticisms of the PCA are numerous, but in my opinion are often misunderstandings that can be challenged. However, perhaps the most pernicious criticism we face is that the PCA is outdated. We can agree that topics and our awareness of them have changed, like gender, power, climate, etc. The world has changed, and our understanding of it has changed, but I don't think that we need to add to the PCA in order to take change into account and be aware of our diversity when encountering another person. As long as I remain in contact and in relation with 'the other', as long as I try to empathically understand the other, as long as I am also willing to change, to congruently communicate, as long as it is not about competing, as long as I retain my way of being, I feel that I can face challenges and I do see the value of the PCA in this time of change and crises in the world.

We can be more self-confident with our approach and our 'way of being with' others and in the outside world. Of course, again and again the current world situation scares me and I doubt that things will turn out well for all of us, but then I get in contact with those who share my values and who do have an effect on others: people who are facing up to the current difficulties, be it by dealing with the current challenges on an academic, philosophical or intellectual level or by accompanying people who are at risk of breaking down due to current challenges and finding ways of dealing with these challenges together.

I don't want to sound naïve and unrealistically optimistic; I am definitely not saying that all will end well as long as we have the 'right' attitude. There are moments when I am frightened by the current world situation but I try to take myself seriously, to connect and stay connected to others, to continue dialogue and help to understand.

Conclusion

The PCA, as an attitude far beyond psychotherapy, stands in contrast to the current mainstream, but that does not necessarily mean that we have to adapt to this mainstream. I would say that the PCA as a political approach is apt and fit to face the present challenges in the world. Be it in a one-on-one setting or on a larger scale. The core idea of the PCA is the relation between persons; so if we keep an ongoing dialogue among all parties that is characterised by respect, authenticity, congruence and empathic understanding, this will not only facilitate personal growth but also the possibility of mutually acceptable solutions. At the present time, this may be more difficult than in Rogers' time, but as soon as I am in contact with people, and I also feel in contact when writing this chapter, I feel supported in my way of being and thinking, leading me to my final thought.

The person-centred approach is not a solution to global challenges, but with a person-centred attitude we are able to facilitate growth and accompanying development, as shown in this book's examples of colleagues' practice. I am convinced that the PCA is still a unique and revolutionary approach, with an offer and contribution to make in a changing and challenging world.

Notes

1 Rogers, C.R., 'The necessary and sufficient conditions of therapeutic personality change', in *Journal of Consulting Psychology* 21, 2, pp. 95–103, 1957
2 Schmid, P.F., 'Psychotherapy is political or it is not psychotherapy: The person-centered approach as an essentially political venture', in *Person-Centered and Experiential Psychotherapies*, 11, 2, pp. 95–108, 2012
3 Rogers, 1957
4 Rogers, 1957
5 Biermann-Ratjen, E.-M., Eckert, J. and Schwartz, H.-J., *Gesprächspsychotherapie. Verändern durch Verstehen* (Kohlhammer, 1995)
6 Rogers, C.R., *On Becoming a Person: A Therapist's View of Psychotherapy* (Houghton Mifflin, 1961)
7 Rogers, C.R., 'Client-centered psychotherapy', in Sadock, B.J., Kaplan, H.I., Freedman, A.M., eds., *Comprehensive Textbook of Psychiatry III* (Williams and Wilkins, 1980) pp. 2153–68
8 Schmid, P.F. 'The power of hope: Person-centered perspectives on contemporary personal and societal challenges', in *PCE Journal* 18, 2, pp. 121–38, 2019
9 Schmid, P.F., 2019
10 Schmid, P.F., 'Psychotherapy is political or is not psychotherapy', in *PCE Journal* 11, 2, pp. 95–108, 2012
11 Rogers, C.R., *Carl Rogers on Personal Power: Inner Strength and Its Revolutionary Impact* (Delacorte, 1977)

2 Working with Refugees, Asylum Seekers and Unaccompanied Children in Greece

The Challenges of Working with Global Issues

Alex Vallidis and Elektra Diakolambrianou

It is estimated that about 1.3 million people came to Europe seeking asylum in 2015,[1] the most in a single year since World War II.[2] The vast majority, over 1 million people, entered the European borders by crossing the Mediterranean Sea, most of them fleeing wars and armed conflicts in Syria, Iraq and Afghanistan. Around 85% of the sea arrivals were in Greece via Turkey, as well as several thousand entering Greece via its land borders.[3] It is estimated that from 2015 until today, the people using Greece as an entry point into Europe amount to more than a million, with 37% of them being children.[4]

As a result of the significant influx into Greece and the arising need to manage the asylum processes while at the same time providing basic needs and care to the asylum seekers, a considerable number of people, especially those with social sciences backgrounds, started working in fields such as the Asylum Agency, the International Organisation for Migration (IOM), the UNHCR, as well as several NGOs.[5] Among them were a significant number of person-centred counsellors and psychotherapists, including the authors of this chapter. The year 2015 found Alexandros Vallidis on Samos island, working as a caseworker in an outreach programme for unaccompanied children, and later as the coordinator of a shelter for unaccompanied children with PRAKSIS NGO and Save the Children International. At the same time, Elektra Diakolambrianou was in Athens, working as a guardian for unaccompanied children with METAdrasi NGO.

As a child protection caseworker, Alex was responsible for assessing and handling cases of children at risk of abuse or neglect. He wrote reports, participated in legal procedures and worked closely with families and social services to ensure the safety and well-being of the children. Elektra's responsibilities as a guardian for unaccompanied children included various forms of personalised support and safeguarding of the children's rights and best interests. She was responsible for ensuring their access to asylum and

DOI: 10.4324/9781003536048-4

hospital care, to education and all the activities necessary for their psychosocial development. Both of these were field positions that, despite including counselling elements, were significantly different from the 'traditional' setting of counselling and psychotherapy. In this chapter, we would like to share our experience as person-centred psychotherapists working as field workers; the challenges we faced, but also the ways in which the person-centred approach informed our practice.

During the first phase of the influx, we encountered trauma as we listened to people from entirely different backgrounds, often shaped by very difficult and adverse experiences. Some refugees had experienced war, bombings and conflict, while others fled their countries to avoid impending violence in their regions. Some people left because they could no longer live under the life-threatening conditions related to the economic state of their country. These individuals are often described as migrants seeking better economic opportunities; however, when we focus on the basic needs that must be met for a person to feel safe, we see that most migrants had serious reasons to flee – often connected to unmet basic human rights such as education, public health or extreme poverty.

Additionally, many of these individuals encountered traumatic experiences during their journey, particularly at the hands of traffickers who had promised them safe passage. In the best-case scenario, they found themselves in overcrowded, unsafe boats. Many were also misinformed about their destination, believing, for instance, that the island of Samos was part of the mainland. They were told they would stay on the island for only a few days before being allowed to continue to Europe, but this changed with the closure of the borders in March 2016.[6]

We had to deal with three types of trauma: acute trauma from immediate, distressing experiences; chronic trauma from long-term exposure to traumatic events, often affecting development; and vicarious trauma, as refugees not only recounted their own experiences but also re-experienced traumatic events through communication with relatives over the phone.[7] The impact of this complex trauma was evident in their self-concept. From what we observed, people who have experienced psychological trauma often struggle to maintain a balanced outlook on life. They tend to view their past more negatively while placing higher hopes on the future, possibly as a way to compensate for what they've lost. The extent of post-traumatic growth depends on the intensity of the trauma. Trauma affects more than just emotions; it impacts everything from motivation and willpower to self-esteem, altering how people see their lives and often disrupting their daily routines.[8]

In PCE practice, we prioritise helping clients move from self-concealment to self-disclosure, particularly in cases of trauma. Self-concealment, which is often linked to psychosomatic pain, distress and depression, involves clients hiding their emotions and experiences due to internal stigma.[9] We create a safe, empathic environment where clients feel accepted, allowing them to gradually reveal and process their deeper emotional experiences. Our approach is grounded in unconditional positive regard, providing clients with a non-judgemental space where they can express their vulnerabilities without fear of criticism, which is especially critical when addressing trauma.[10]

Empathy is a cornerstone of our work, fostering trust and supporting clients as they process their trauma symbolically and create personal meaning from their experiences.[11] We also emphasise congruence, ensuring that we, as therapists, have processed our own losses and can differentiate our experiences from those of the client, thereby preventing burnout and enhancing the therapeutic relationship.[12] Additionally, we assist clients in regulating their emotions and integrating their trauma into their self-concept, recognising that refugees often struggle with emotional dysregulation and intrusive thoughts.[13] Our therapeutic space is designed to be free from external pressure, allowing clients to explore their trauma organically and at their own pace.[14] Finally, we support the continuation of meaningful connections with the trauma, guiding clients in finding purpose within their experiences, which can prevent complications in the healing process.[15]

A common phenomenon observed in the context of the refugee crisis was vicarious trauma, which affected not only the refugees themselves but also the cultural mediators and professionals involved in providing assistance. Cultural mediators faced a particularly difficult position, as they navigated the dual identities of being refugees and helpers, while professionals, who were accustomed to stable environments, encountered something entirely new. In Greece, a country that had recently faced an economic crisis but not political unrest, these challenges were especially pronounced. It is essential to differentiate between two types of trauma that emerged: Secondary Traumatic Stress (STS) and Vicarious Trauma (VT). STS refers to the emotional and psychological effects of indirectly experiencing trauma through helping or empathising with trauma survivors, manifesting as similar to PTSD with symptoms such as intrusive thoughts, hyperarousal and avoidance behaviours.[16] VT, however, emphasises the cumulative impact of prolonged exposure to trauma through empathetic engagement, leading to significant alterations in the helper's cognitive schemas and perceptions of safety, trust and control, ultimately disrupting their worldview and belief systems.[17] This shift in belief within the person can ultimately impact their positive paradigm and person-centred identity. To safeguard this, individuals need to invest in personal growth and seek supervision.

Another one of the challenges we encountered was burnout. The factors leading to that were in fact numerous, and most often organisational rather than individual. Most of the field workers, mental health professionals, social workers, educators, etc., were essentially finding themselves in front of quite unique challenges and dilemmas, without necessarily having had adequate specialised training on how to face them. Apart from the multiple and repeated layers of trauma,[18] they also had to deal with major cultural and language barriers, which were not always overcome through the intervention of interpreters and mediators; mental health workers in particular were faced with the need to reconsider their idea of what therapy should be like. More often than not, the ideological presuppositions of dominant psychology proved to be too Western and colonial to be helpful, thus underlining the necessity for a more pluralistic mosaic of multi-layered approaches, what Mantzari & Mentinis distinctively refer to as 'borderland psychologies'.[19] At the same time, the job descriptions and demands were often making the lines between personal involvement and professional detachment very blurry, rendering it very difficult to protect one's professional boundaries.[20] In addition to that, the lack of resources as well as the bureaucracy that characterises the field often led to feelings of disappointment, powerlessness and job dissatisfaction.[21] The combination of these factors, along with the demanding hours and intense workplace conditions, led to significantly increased work-related stress[22] and burnout[23] among the refugee-aid workers.

From a person-centred and experiential (PCE) perspective, we emphasise the preventive factors within our paradigm for therapists working in a shared trauma context. Central to this approach is the growth paradigm of the person-centred approach, which contrasts with the traditional dualistic clinical model by proposing a mutual growth framework for both therapist and client.[24] Congruence in person-centred therapy fosters a deep connection between therapist and client, leading to compassion satisfaction, which is recognised as a protective factor.[25] Moreover, by placing empathy, rather than compassion, at the heart of the therapeutic process, we trust in the person's inherent healing capacities, thereby alleviating the therapist from assuming responsibility for the client's life or bearing the burden of unresolved issues, such as war.[26] Holding space for difficult emotions can create a sense of connection with the client, grounding both in the present moment.[27]

Accurate symbolisation of experience and unconditional positive regard can, in turn, foster a relational space where the client can recognise emerging emotions, the different configurations of the self and their importance in navigating trauma and crisis.[28] In situations where everything is at stake, both the client and the counsellor can rely on their self-structure, which mutually leans towards growth. Moreover, in terms of supervision, the counsellor recognises the functioning therapist rather than striving for the ideal therapist who is expected to be perfect under any circumstances; a process that is equally essential for the prevention and management of burnout.

Indeed, the person-centred therapeutic and supervisory relationship can help the therapist to openly process and reflect on their work-related pressures within a framework devoid of criticism and performance anxiety, thus facilitating them to reintegrate their alienated sense of self and to increase their resilience towards current and future challenges.[29] In a recent study on the experience of burnout among person-centred therapists in Greece,[30] all participants reported that burnout led them to a deteriorated sense of self as well as a difficulty in maintaining their presence in the therapeutic process, both of which often prevented them from sufficiently providing their clients with the necessary therapeutic conditions. At the same time, however, all participants also highlighted the power of supervision and personal therapy as protective factors against burnout. More imperatively though, they emphasised the need for educational modules on burnout prevention and self-care in the training programmes of future person-centred psychotherapists.

Ten years after the peak of the refugee 'crisis' in Europe, the year 2025 finds the authors of this chapter in different working positions. However, our current professional activities are certainly influenced by our experiences in the refugee-aid field, and, not by chance, strongly focused on person-centred psychotherapy training. Elektra spent two years working in a Erasmus+ Cooperation Partnership programme aiming to develop burnout prevention and self-care tools for 'professional dreamers', including a self-care card deck,[31] a methodology of experiential exercises for groups,[32] as well as a series of interviews about burnout.[33] She recently presented these tools at the 16th World Conference of Person-Centred and Experiential Counselling and Psychotherapy in Athens, linking them to the PCE approach and showcasing the ways in which they can be implemented and integrated within PCE practice.[34] Meanwhile, Alexandros is currently exploring the application of person-centred and experiential counselling for relational trauma, working with refugee children who have survived gender-based violence, with a focus on fostering a safe and supportive environment for healing.[35] Moreover, he is developing empathic mapping as a means of ensuring that the refugee maintains control of the experience, while the counsellor focuses on experiential specificity and intensifies the communication of empathy to the client.[36]

Adopting a person-centred philosophy within an organisational culture can help reduce burnout by addressing workload and bureaucracy, placing the practitioner at the centre and promoting relational satisfaction through meaningful connections.[37] This approach supports compassion satisfaction, which is linked to lower levels of burnout, by ensuring practitioners have the time, energy and conditions to engage in quality relationships. Including the therapist as a person and prioritising their psychological well-being enhances emotional resilience and helps sustain compassionate care.

Notes

1 Barlai, M., Fähnrich, B., Griessler, C. and Rhomberg, M. (eds) *The Migrant crisis: European perspectives and national discourses* (LIT, 2017)
2 Dumont, J.C. and Scarpet, S., 'Is this humanitarian migration crisis different?' in *Migration Policy Debates* (OECD, September 2015)
3 IOM 'Irregular Migrant, Refugee Arrivals in Europe Top One Million in 2015'. IOM. 22 December 2015
4 UNHCR., 'Facts and Statistics' *Global Trends Report*, 2023. www.unhcr.org/global-trends

5 Cusumano, E. and Pattison, J., 'The Non-Governmental Provision of Search and Rescue in the Mediterranean and the Abdication of State Responsibility' in *Cambridge Review of International Affairs* 31 (1), 2 January 2018 pp. 53–75

6 Weber, L., 'The Impact of Border Closures on Refugee Mobility' in *Journal of Migration Studies* 14, 2017 pp. 203–10

7 Even, D., Marcus, G. and Shira, R., 'Chronic Trauma and Its Impact on Development' in *Journal of Child Development* 35, 2024 pp. 101–20

8 Spytska, L., 'Psychological Trauma and Its Influence on Daily Life' in *Mental Health Review* 29, 2023 pp. 45–67

9 Larson, D.G. and Chastain, R., 'Self-Concealment: Conceptualization, Measurement, and Health Implications' in *Journal of Social and Clinical Psychology* 9, 1990 pp. 439–55

10 Larson, D.G., 'A Person-Centered Approach to Grief Counseling', in *The handbook of person-centered psychotherapy and counseling* by M. Cooper, M. O'Hara, P.F. Schmid, and A. Bohart (eds) (London: Palgrave Macmillan, 2013) pp. 313–26

11 Knox, J., '"Feeling for" and "Feeling with": Developmental and Neuroscientific Perspectives on Intersubjectivity and Empathy' in *Journal of Analytical Psychology* 58, 2013 pp. 491–509

12 Larson, D.G., 'A Person-Centered Approach to Grief Counseling', 2013

13 Warner, M.S., 'Process with Difficult Clients', in *The handbook of person-centered psychotherapy and counseling* by M. Cooper, M. O'Hara, P.F. Schmid, and A. Bohart (eds) (London: Palgrave Macmillan, 2013) pp. 343–58

14 Larson, D.G., 'A Person-Centered Approach to Grief Counseling', 2013

15 Klass, D., *Continuing bonds: New understandings of grief* (Taylor & Francis, 2006)

16 Sprang, G., Ford, J., Kerig, P. and Bride, B., 'Defining Secondary Traumatic Stress and Developing Targeted Assessments and Interventions: Lessons Learned from Research and Leading Experts' in *Traumatology* 25 (2), 2019 pp. 72–81. https://doi.org/10.1037/trm0000185

17 Branson, D.C., 'Vicarious Trauma, Themes in Research, and Terminology: A Review of Literature' in *Traumatology* 25 (1), 2019 p. 2. https://doi.org/10.1037/trm0000161

18 Borho, A., Georgiadou, E. and Grimm, T. and others 'Professional and Volunteer Refugee Aid Workers-Depressive Symptoms and Their Predictors, Experienced Traumatic Events, PTSD, Burdens, Engagement Motivators and Support Needs' in *International Journal of Environmental Research and Public Health* 16 (22), 17 November 2019 p. 4542

19 Mantzari, D. and Mentinis, M. (eds) *Borderland psychologies: Mapping gray areas of mental healthcare for refugees* (Oposito, 2024)

20 Gemignani, M. and Giliberto, M., 'Constructions of Burnout, Identity, and Self-Care in Professionals Working toward the Psychosocial Care of Refugees and Asylum Seekers in Italy' in *Journal of Constructivist Psychology* 34 (1) 2020 pp. 1–23.

21 Lymperis, P., '*Aspects and dimensions of work-related stress: Burnout and job satisfaction of employees of the Ministry of Immigration and Asylum* [Master thesis] University of West Attica, School of Administrative, Economic and Social Sciences, Athens, Greece, 2021

22 Ntavara, E.N., *Work-related stress in Refugee Shelters – Case Study at the Reception and Identification Centers of the country* [Master thesis] University of West Attica, School of Administrative, Economic and Social Sciences, Athens, Greece, 2022

23 Alexandri, S., *Stress and burnout of workers in accommodation facilities for refugees* [Master thesis] Hellenic Open University, School of Social Sciences, Patras, Greece, 2022

24 Stephen, J. and Murphy, D., 'Person-Centered Approach, Positive Psychology, and Relational Helping: Building Bridges' in *Journal of Humanistic Psychology* 53 (1), 2013 pp. 26–51

25 Rothschild, B., *Help for the helper: The psychophysiology of compassion fatigue and vicarious trauma* (WW Norton & Company, 2006)
26 Rogers, C.R., *Client-centered therapy: Its current practice, implications, and theory* (Houghton Mifflin, 1951)
27 Tolan, J., *Skills in person-centred counselling & psychotherapy* (SAGE Publications 2012)
28 Mearns, D. and Cooper, M., *Working at relational depth in counselling and psychotherapy* (SAGE Publications, 2005)
29 Monokrousou, A., *Person-centered psychotherapy, stress and burnout in working with refugees* [Master thesis]. ICPS College of Humanistic Sciences, Athens, Greece, 2024
30 Koniou, K., *Burnout of person-centered psychotherapists and its impact on the effectiveness of therapy and on the psychotherapeutic conditions* [Master thesis] ICPS College of Humanistic Sciences, Athens, Greece, 2024
31 Spikey's Clinic for Professional Dreamers: *Spikey's Deck of Remedies*, 2024
32 Spikey's Clinic for Professional Dreamers: *The Methodology*, 2024
33 Spikey's Clinic for Professional Dreamers: *Youtube Channel*, 2024
34 Diakolambrianou, E., 'Spikey's Deck of Remedies: Preventing burnout through play' *Workshop at the 16th World Conference of Person-Centered and Experiential Counseling and Psychotherapy*, Athens, 9–13/10/2024
35 Vallidis, A., 'Person-centered and experiential counselling for relational trauma' *[Conference presentation] Presented at the 16th World Conference of Person-Centered and Experiential Counseling and Psychotherapy,* Athens, 9–13/10/2024
36 Vallidis, A., *Person-centered and experiential counseling for relational trauma* (UNHCR, 2025, in press)
37 Raina, R., 'Moving Crisis to Opportunities: A Corporate Perspective on the Impact of Compassionate Empathic Behaviour on the Well-Being of Employees' in *International Journal of Global Business and Competitiveness* 17 (2), 2022 pp. 239–55

3 Applying the Person-Centred Approach in a Time of War

Working across Modalities to Deliver Support and Supervision to Those in a War Zone

Mairi McMenamin and Terry Daly

Russia's invasion of Ukraine in February 2022 sent shock waves around the world. Like many others, we sat in stunned helplessness while watching evacuations to the west, conscriptions of men to fight and the bombing of Ukrainian cities unfold.

We had an opportunity to confront our feelings of powerlessness and horror in the face of this conflict when a call went out to therapists across Europe for supervision to be offered to psychologists working in Ukraine. We had both made connections with Ukrainian therapists at conferences and workshops and were keen to help so these positive, prior encounters became our foundation for offering support in a time of crisis.

This chapter reflects on how we, two person-centred therapists from Scotland, supported a group of Gestalt-trained Ukrainian psychologists. These psychologists were dealing with profound trauma, both from working with clients directly affected by the conflict and from their own personal experiences of loss and fear. At the time this group was working, ideas were circulating that the person-centred approach (PCA) was not relevant in a time of crisis and that it did not apply to trauma. We assert here that our experience suggests otherwise.

The Elements of Person-Centred Supervision

When PCE Europe, a network of person-centred and experiential psychotherapists and counsellors, put out a call for therapists to provide supervision to Ukrainian psychologists we responded, at first independently but soon agreed to work together. We are experienced practitioners and supervisors who have worked closely together for over 20 years. Because of a deep connection to each other, having worked at depth for so long, we offer each other the core conditions and have a profound psychological contact when we work together. We focus

DOI: 10.4324/9781003536048-5

on our relationship with each other, not only those we are working with. This connection facilitates therapeutic presence, which emerged as fundamental in setting the conditions for the work that unfolded in this group.

For us, person-centred supervision is about the individual bringing all of themselves to supervision and the value of this focus on the therapist themselves. However, while the initial request was for supervision, it soon became clear that the greatest need was for emotional support and a safe space for the Ukrainian psychologists who, at that time, were overwhelmed by the trauma they were witnessing and experiencing. We felt confident that the PCA was a perfect fit because of its non-directive stance, connection to dialogue and building of relationships.[1] Within the PCA we would offer the core conditions of empathy, unconditional positive regard (UPR) and congruence to people bringing issues of conflict, fear, uncertainty and hatred in order to provide a space where they could process these complex emotions and not be judged.

Rogers' basic theory is grounded in a non-directive stance, 'the politics of the person-centred approach is a conscious renunciation of and avoidance of all control over, or decision-making for the client', thus allowing the client to direct themself.[2] For us, the non-directive simply means the belief that the 'other' has, if given the right conditions, vast resources within themselves, and we do not take the lead in directing the discovery of these resources, or inadvertently block the individual learning about self.

Thus, we, with the help of an interpreter, established a supervision and support group. Initially envisaged as a ten-week group for emotional support rather than what would be deemed traditional supervision, at the request of the group, it first extended to fortnightly then monthly meetings over a period of 18 months. It quickly became a safe place for these psychologists to express their emotions and share their struggles in a non-judgmental, empathic environment with the ability to remain open to and respect difference.

The Challenges of Applying the PCA in a Time of War

The challenges of being a person-centred practitioner and applying the PCA in this context were immediately obvious in a group where all the therapists who attended were directly impacted by the war, identified themselves as Gestalt-trained therapists and came from a different culture. Communication was immediately challenged by different perspectives on the purpose of the group, a different language and a culturally different way of expressing experience; verbally, emotionally and in the context of their country's history of conflict and war.

The Impact of War

From the outset it was clear that these psychologists were working to offer emotional support to clients whilst traumatised themselves; this was reflected by a group member who observed that the so called 'normal' ways of responding do not explain individual responses in a crisis. A few of the psychologists in the group expressed a growing understanding that there was 'no safe place' and, most powerfully, 'nowhere to run'. This was at a time when some were working with individuals sheltering in tunnels or with soldiers on the frontline, others were trying to continue to work in clinics where all around them bombs were being dropped. This, alongside each individual therapist dealing with their own response to the war, fear for their families and often loss of husbands, fathers, brothers and lovers to the fighting.

As supervisors, it was vital to acknowledge this in the group and to communicate empathy and UPR to allow the group members to bring their own fears to supervision as well as their client work. For us, this was 'encounter' in its broadest sense, as defined by Rogers.[3] The unfolding of openness, dialogue and reflection on self were enormously beneficial to the group and were evidence of how applying the conditions of the PCA effects change, both in individuals and in a group.

For us too the impact of war and of witnessing the trauma and fear experienced by the psychologists was profound. We felt powerlessness in the early stages of the group but, despite this, remained acutely aware of the need to be fully present with both the group and ourselves in order to be able to support these therapists. Our own personal supervision was crucial in enabling this group as it allowed us to look after ourselves while in the process of the work.

Working across Modalities

As the group progressed and members started to trust that this was a 'safe enough' space, more were able to share their theoretical perspectives, the differences and commonalities between Gestalt and person-centred theory, and some of their own personal struggles and journeys. In truth, we experienced more in common than difference. It became evident, and was increasingly voiced by the group, that they were working to stay with their understanding of their own theory but were able to express the value of experiencing the person-centred offering of the core conditions.

The Language Barrier

Working with a group whose first language was Ukrainian also brought some challenges. Even though some group members spoke English, they initially lacked the confidence to speak in the group. Our Ukrainian contact had identified an interpreter for us and a strong, effective working relationship soon developed with them. It was clear that our interpreter, whilst not person-centred trained, shared our person-centred values and that they were also greatly in need of support as they too were working in shock, fear and anxiety for the future.

They too were traumatised by the war but recognised the need to hold their feelings in check in order to be authentic in interpreting what others were expressing. 'As an interpreter, I've experienced how our minds work differently when doing this job. It's challenging, requiring both mental effort to focus on the group dialogue and emotional detachment to allow me to interpret directly what is being said'. We recognised this and supported them to hold their reactions while in the group, to allow them to interpret accurately. In their words,

> … detachment, however, can lead to internal struggles as I know from experience that I need to hold my own perspectives. My therapist gave me a helpful mantra, "I am here to interpret from language to language without getting emotionally involved"

As supervisors we managed this, talked about it and offered debriefing sessions before and after each group session. This proved to be invaluable for all three of us and helped the interpreter navigate their own emotions; freed them from their emotional reactions and allowed them to focus on what was being said. Debriefing provided for them what supervision did for us; it ensured we could each be fully present whilst allowing ourselves to witness the full horror of what was unfolding.

For us as supervisors, it was clear from the beginning of the process that in order to tackle these challenges we would need to offer the six necessary and sufficient conditions to maintain psychological contact, be non-directive in attitude, listen closely to each expression of emotion, sometimes check out group members' understanding, express some of what was 'not being said' or, what was defined by Rogers as, 'on the edge of the client's awareness'[4] and to give time for the supervisee to take this in and respond. This required us to be fully present and often felt very powerful. For example, one therapist who started to bring her own fears and emotions to the group said they would never take this to supervision in their own modality. When asked why they felt this they said, 'I would be judged, and that would silence me'.

Change and Growth through Encounter

It is challenging to describe the content of the supervision group process, not just for reasons of confidentiality but also because of the complex and evolving shared reality of group members. However, it included exploration of the fragmentation of family and family life; the loss of core relationships such as husbands, fathers, brothers, lovers; the distress of having to uproot from your own country; leaving others behind and trying to establish yourself in a new culture with a new language. As the group's honesty and connection grew it was recognised that the current trauma was connected to transgenerational trauma, as their country had experienced collective trauma from previous wars and political upheaval.[5] This had created a deep fear, a strong sense of powerlessness and acknowledgment of 'being in survival mode'.

When the group first met in the summer of 2022, this sense of powerlessness was palpable. Our psychologists were trying to manage their own fear, loss and instability while, at the same time, supporting clients who were also in trauma. At these early stages, some wanted to focus on having 'a guide'; for one, who was feeling lost, this was her 'Northern Star'. Their focus was on the client's trauma but slowly, they started to explore with us the boundaries to be identified between them and their clients, the emerging therapeutic relationships and their experience of trying to offer empathy and UPR in a time of crisis. This work was complex and demanded accurate focus from the facilitators.

By October 2022, anger and sometimes rage at the Russian attacks began to be talked about. This emerged as a complex issue as some group members did not agree with reflections on 'Russians' as different. Some group members expressed difficulty in dealing with Russian aggression, both in the therapy room and as it infiltrated their family lives. One therapist described her alarm when a client arrived with a gun. The client needed to talk but was unable to feel safe without a gun on her person. The members of the group held differing views on how to manage this, but the scenario allowed dialogue to emerge and differences to be acknowledged. The therapist explained that, after speaking with the client, the work had continued as the client agreed to have the gun unloaded while in the therapy room. Some group members were able to voice experiencing the level of violence they witnessed as 'a cancerous illness', this enabled them to offer unconditionality to their clients, allowing them to hold their reality and to continue to work with this level of dissonance in the client.

It also began to be evident that the therapists themselves were noticing the need to 'manage' their own anger in order to be present to clients. Several group sessions began to focus on self-care. The success of the approach here was that the process of offering the core conditions of the PCA allowed individuals to voice their fears and to have these heard and validated. One member of the group, after many weeks, was able to share that she had experienced an assault. Her experience of receiving empathy, unconditionality and a non-directive attitude from the group allowed her to feel safe to say more and to contribute to dialogue in the group. There would be more work for this individual to process in the future, but, in that moment, the value of her feelings being expressed and heard was visibly supportive. This focus on self-care was expressed as a helpful process for some, which allowed them to continue to work whilst still being afraid daily.

By January 2023, discussions had moved to a sense of separation. Some therapists had by then fled to other countries but continued to engage with the group. Sometimes people managed to listen in on the group but were not able to use their video because it wasn't safe. For some, being in Ukraine was articulated as easier than running because they had some sense of control;

outside their own country, they felt they had no control. Literally, they described this as 'fleeing'. The focus for us as facilitators was the ability to be responsive to whatever supervisees brought and wherever they were working from. There was flexibility in time boundaries and the rules of engagement, whilst retaining respect for each other and the holding of confidentiality.

A non-directive attitude was key to allowing emotion to be processed with no judgement. Giving and receiving empathy and authenticity were also evident in this group. Group participants experienced change and growth in themselves with a new appreciation of Rogers' work. As one said, 'Rogers' idea that "what is most personal, is most universal" really made sense to me. Rogers' perspectives provide a solid foundation for understanding people and creating an environment that supports personal growth'.

Although originally envisaged as a ten-week group, we kept the door open to everybody until it was no longer needed. The group came to a natural end in March 2024, once people had established new avenues of supervision and support within their new situations and countries.

Conclusion

This group reaffirmed for us that the PCA is applicable in times of crisis, conflict and war because it provides a space of trust, empathy, congruence and emotional safety. It gave these psychologists the freedom to be themselves whilst grappling with their traumatic experiences and helped them continue their work with many traumatised individuals. This group emphasised that the PCA's six necessary and sufficient conditions are crucial in helping support individuals and communities, even in testing times. This work confirmed the relevance of working in a therapeutic relationship that values authenticity, a non-directive attitude and therapeutic presence, where presence here was an overarching condition for change alongside the six conditions.[6]

The theoretical basis of non-directivity comes from a belief in the actualising tendency towards growth.[7] In the 18 months, this group worked together, the tendency to growth was felt tangibly by both facilitators and group members. The following words from Iryna,[8] a group member, captures this,

> Initially, I felt an overwhelming amount of hatred, rage, horror, shame, and guilt. I cried and reacted intensely, feeling unprofessional and incompetent. However, the facilitators surrounded us with acceptance, interest, and support, which quickly alleviated my shame and gave me hope. I am inspired by […] the excellent methodology of the client-centred approach, which emphasises sincerity, congruence, unconditional positive regard, and empathetic understanding. This approach helped me recover quickly, adapt to a new country, gain professional recognition in Great Britain, and build a larger practice within two years of the war.

The experience in Ukraine demonstrates for the authors that the person-centred approach is not merely relevant in times of crisis but essential because it taps into the core of human resilience and the capacity for growth. As we write, the war is not over and survival remains the focus of therapists and clients alike. Although sometimes dismissed by others as a passive approach, here the PCA offered a powerful and transformational response to trauma. Rogers' work in conflict zones like Northern Ireland and South Africa[9] offers a precedent for its effectiveness; this experience shows its ongoing relevance.

We are grateful to our interpreter for their contribution to this chapter but, as the war is on-going, they wish to remain anonymous.

Notes

1 Rogers, C.R., 'The necessary and sufficient conditions of therapeutic personality change' in *Journal of Consulting Psychology*, 21 (2) (1957) pp. 95–103

2 Cissna, K. and Anderson, R., *Moments of meeting: Buber, rogers, and the potential for public dialogue*, p. 98 (State University of New York Press, 2002)

3 Rogers, C.R., 'The interpersonal relationship: The core of guidance' in Rogers, C.R. and Stevens, B., eds. *Person to Person: The problem of being human, a new trend in psychology* pp. 89–104 (Real People Press, 1967)

4 Rogers, C.R., *Client centred therapy; its current practice, implications and theory* (Houghton-Mifflin, 1951)

5 Bezo, B. and Maggi, S, 'Living in "survival mode" Intergenerational transmission of trauma from the Holodomor genocide of 1932–1933' in *Social Science & Medicine*, 134 (2015) pp. 87–94

6 Natiello, P., 'Therapeutic presence: An essential way of being' in Di Malta, G., Cooper, M., O'Hara, M. Gololob, Y. and Stephen, S. *The handbook of person-centred psychotherapy and counselling*, 3rd ed. pp. 226–38, (Bloomsbury, 2024)

7 Geller, S.M. and Greenberg, L.S., 'Therapeutic presence: Therapists' experience of presence in the psychotherapeutic encounter' in *Person-Centred and Experiential Psychotherapies*, 1 (1–2) (2002) pp. 71–86

8 Sachenko, I., *Personal communication* (London, 17 June 2024)

9 Rogers, C.R., *A way of being* (Houghton-Mifflin, 1980)

Section 2

The Person-Centred Approach and Social Change

4 Applying the Person-Centred Approach to a Recruitment Crisis in Social Care

Terry Daly and Kate Munro

Like so many institutions in the UK, the stories about social care are extreme, ranging from touchy-feely wonderfulness to Dickensian horror with untold cruelty. The societal platitudes and rhetoric around social care are equally steeped in incongruence with both a willingness to look away while, at the same time, saying how shocking it is. As a result, social care services seem to be perpetually in a state of crisis over funding, recruitment or quality of care.

This chapter describes a person-centred response to a crisis in the recruitment of social care workers experienced in the late 1990s. However, challenges in recruiting and developing staff who can meet the complexity of providing social care which reflects the values and principles of a civilised society are a recurring problem. Social care agencies repeatedly find themselves struggling to find competent, caring individuals to spearhead the care they provide.

As former social care workers we are acutely aware of the dichotomy that underpins society's view of social care and social care workers. Pushed to prominence during the pandemic, carers were thanked, lauded and admired for the difficult, demanding and highly personal work they do. However, society remains largely unaware of the nature of that work and fails to recognise it in terms of pay, conditions or opportunities for advancement. We maintain a constant denial of this reality, and in the theory of the person-centred approach (PCA), a collective incongruence. Social care workers remain a largely ignored and devalued workforce but nevertheless, one which we rely on in times of our greatest need.

In Scotland, we developed a training programme for social care staff that applied Rogers' six conditions[1] within the theory of the PCA. A programme within which everybody grew and thrived; care workers, clients and the institutions that created structures for support. This is an example of a radical approach with, what may appear to be significant, costs. However, when the principles of the PCA are put into practice and relationships are built something wondrous can happen. This was the case with the Higher Education Certificate in Person-Centred Approaches to Social Care; a partnership of many people from different modalities who believed in the importance of a

DOI: 10.4324/9781003536048-7

quality training package and worked for many years to create and implement a programme that led to a highly cost-effective solution to the recruitment crisis.

In his theory of growth Carl Rogers[2] was able to capture what is essentially best about humanity. The PCA, in our view, is simply a reflection of how we behave when we are safe, secure and eager to grow. It is transformational when it allows us to accept ourselves, which is an incredibly challenging task, as then we can accept others as they are without expecting them to change. This is an essential part of what needs to exist in social care as, in essence, you cannot care for others unless you can care for yourself. Sadly, this is missing much of the time because of the huge expectations on workers and the appalling lack of resources.

In the Beginning

This programme, which would grow into a significant and recognised award, began quietly. We were asked to provide a two-day training course on sex and sexuality in disability services. We developed a programme focussed on relationships, consent and needs, and set about working with a fairly typical group of staff. All were mature students; most were women; all had experience, some significant experience, of working in social care; many had had a poor experience of formal education; some were resistant to training, expecting it to deliver little of practical help; and all had demanding schedules into which they were fitting these two days.

So far, so usual but, as we began to delve into relationships something unexpected happened. These competent, articulate care workers started to talk about how they felt when working with people who needed intimate, personal care. In the safe setting of the training group, they talked about their role in the care relationship, their feelings and their concerns. The discussions were frank and open, so much so that a neighbouring meeting started loudly singing *Onward Christian Soldiers* – presumably in an attempt to drown out our candid, animated discussions of masturbation, unwanted touching and sexual attraction! Our shared laughter helped the participants to further relax and open up about their emotional reactions at work. This was a pivotal moment as Terry, by then an accomplished person-centred therapist and lecturer, recognised within this group an implicit understanding of their role in the caring relationship and the tools that could help them deliver supportive, growthful relationships.

The Need for a Person-Centred Approach

The course received glowing, positive feedback and armed with this we met with the consortium of social care providers, Altrum, that had sponsored the course. At that time Altrum comprised seven organisations providing supported living services to vulnerable adults. Their services were designed and delivered according to the individual's unique needs and wishes; there was no 'one size fits all' model. Their staff were unqualified but experienced, involved in the often complex and demanding role of offering individualised support, usually in one-to-one settings, isolated from managers and colleagues.

Altrum were frustrated at the perceived inadequacy of the training available at that time but had no clear idea of what was needed to supplement it. They employed experienced competent staff who knew all about lifting and handling, community mapping, operating wheelchairs etc. The gap in their training was not in terms of practicalities, it was in their levels of self-awareness and self-acceptance, which directly impacted what they were able to bring to the caring relationship and how they could use themselves in caring for others.

We believed they needed to know, understand and apply the PCA. By offering the core conditions of empathy, congruence and unconditional positive regard to these staff they would, in turn, begin to better understand and accept themselves, and, in doing so, be more accepting of others. Thus, they would be able to form genuine, quality relationships with their clients. The application of the PCA allowed us to articulate one further shared, though not always consciously known, value, we and Altrum each recognised that the greatest resource available to the support worker was the self.

The Teaching Programme

With the backing of Altrum we were able to think big and soon the 'course' had developed into three, three-day courses. These three, which became the core modules of the programme, were:

- Understanding Self: during which students learned about transition,[3] the Johari Window[4] and the core conditions of the person-centred approach[5]
- Active Listening: exploring the core conditions and how they could be practised in social care
- Understanding Others: designed to integrate with the first two, this module explored PCA theory,[6] transactional analysis[7] and ego states[8]

Altrum, meanwhile, had also been thinking big and had secured funding from the European Social Fund for the programme. With this they were able to develop three further modules related to person centred planning tools. Four existing courses that focused on the complex nature of the support relationship were then integrated into the programme and a final two modules returned to the theme of the professional role of social care workers exploring the individual, the group and the team and the reflective practitioner.

The final partner to join the programme was Queen Margaret University, Edinburgh. With an established reputation for excellence in the teaching of health, rehabilitation and social services, it was the obvious choice as a supervising and awarding body. Queen Margaret judged the programme to be a Certificate of Higher Education or Higher National Certificate (HNC). This university award met a key aim that Altrum held when entering into the development process; a formal qualification that taught that good care was defined by a quality caring relationship.

The Core Conditions in Action

Key to this programme was a recognition that this was a very particular group of students. These individuals performed quality, demanding work but often with little formal education and scant on-going training. The design of the programme needed to recognise their two contradictory sides. On the one hand, they had a rich experience of working with people, would problem-solve every day, held down challenging jobs and had a wide variety of life skills and experiences. However, they were also returning to learning as mature students, many had negative experiences of education and had been away from formal education for a long time.

From the start, we knew that this programme should not only teach but also model the PCA. This included, but also extended beyond, offering the core conditions in all interactions with students. The core conditions needed to be applied to the design, structure and delivery of the programme. Because of their prior, poor experience in formal learning settings these students needed a level of care, support and empathy seldom seen in large-scale training enterprises. However, the innate understanding of the PCA demonstrated in their practice alongside their professional competence gave us confidence that they would recognise and respond to this modelling.

Person-Centredness in Teaching

Using empathy and active listening we designed a teaching programme that acknowledged the hesitancy, anxiety and, in some cases, fear that students held about learning. The teaching strategy was grounded in unconditional positive regard, seeking to provide students with a non-judgemental space where they could express their ideas, questions and vulnerabilities without fear of criticism. Within this they could raise their personal prejudices and struggles to accept difference within the group, knowing these would be met with understanding from the programme team. This often resulted in significant shifts to more accepting attitudes on the part of students.

Teaching methods in the first module were reflective, organised around large group work and individual tasks, with lots of practical activities, but little exposure of individuals or their ideas. In the second module, students were ready to try small group work and pairs practice to begin to develop their skills in active listening, empathy, congruence and UPR. By the third course, training techniques including modelling and role play were being used; the levels of trust and confidence within the group now being relatively high.

Perhaps one of the main characteristics of the teaching programme was its encouragement of adult relationships with student-led learning outcomes. In practice, this meant students taking a lead in their own learning, actively exploring ways in which they could embrace the theory from their own point of view and giving and receiving feedback to each other and trainers consistent with the values of the PCA.

A Person-Centred Assessment Process

Assessment distinguished this programme from other training courses. Students were required to produce quality, academic assignments that demonstrated their learning and ability to apply that learning. However, given the student's past experience, it was essential that this university-standard assessment process was not only fair, valid and reliable but also person-centred.

A range of flexible and responsive measures were put in place to assist students who could be resistant to or disempowered by assessments. These included written assignments, which could be oral presentations, self and peer assessment, class presentations and observed practice in the workplace. Early modules included worked examples of assignments to guide students while on-going support from workplace mentors aimed to minimise the perceived scale of the task and to overcome any reluctance to ask for help.

Detailed feedback on assignments was provided by trainers. This feedback was particularly important if an assignment did not meet the pass criteria. Students had multiple opportunities to re-submit, receiving taped 'teaching' feedback to help them produce quality work.

The results were a joy. Students with little or no experience of further education produced competent, insightful work. Within the conditions of the course, they were able to create a safe space for themselves to learn, question and reflect. Central to this was our unconditional acceptance of them as students. Their work was transformative, both in our perceptions of what they could achieve and in their confidence in their ability to study, learn and apply complex ideas and concepts. At the beginning of the first module, students were guarded, wary and anxious but following their first assignment they were open, cautiously optimistic and questioning; they were beginning to shape their own learning.

Supporting Students in a Person-Centred Way

As must be obvious by now, this programme could not have been developed or sustained without considerable investment in terms of time, money and resources from Altrum and its constituent members. The programme would not have worked without their willingness to support their staff in both attending the programme and in integrating their learning back into the workplace.

The programme was integrated into regular supervision and mentors offered support, as did fellow team members who themselves were past students. Individual support encouraged self-awareness, helping students to identify their barriers to learning and the ways in which they could be removed. This was evidenced by the congruent relationships that developed between students and the programme team; a team that, over time, grew to include Altrum staff and clients in teaching, mentoring and the assessment of practice.

Outcomes of the Programme

Collaboration between trainers, employers and the awarding body was key to the success of the programme. Each brought their own skills, ideas and agendas and these dovetailed to ensure the best possible results. Outcomes were measured in staff retention, levels of caring skills and the ability to work with a strong sense of ethics and accountability.

For Altrum, the outcomes met their initial aims and hopes for the programme. They now had an accredited, formal qualification that met their needs as employers and was recognised by the Scottish Social Services Council (SSSC). They developed a highly qualified, enquiring, confident, open group of staff who increasingly took on leadership roles. As a consortium of social care employers there was reduced risk of losing these newly qualified and energised staff; many would move on but often to other members of the consortia thus reducing the attrition often seen in organisations who pay for but don't benefit from newly trained staff.

In the 12 years that the programme ran, over 700 students, including 3 service users, achieved not only increased skills but also transformed attitudes, acceptance and relationships. It took almost three years for students to complete the programme; three years of training, reading, assignments, workplace observation, mentoring and supervision. However, despite the extended commitment required, the rate of attrition was low. Over the course of three years students would get sick, have babies, change jobs etc. but they would return to the programme, always aiming to complete. On completion, they were able to demonstrate a range of person-centred skills, engage learning strategies to benefit their professional development and master the therapeutic conditions.

However, outcomes were not only seen in the workplace, what became evident was very powerful evidence of personal growth and development. Feedback from students was as much about personal as it was professional growth. Students talked about the journey of self-acceptance and an internalisation of the locus of evaluation with resulting growth in self-esteem. The authors believe that if we are to deal with the crisis in social care we have to view these personal outcomes as valuable, albeit harder to measure than professional or organisational goals.

External recognition came from, among others, Queen Margaret University, the Scottish Consortium for Learning Disabilities, a National Training Award and a European Social Fund Good Practice Award for Lifelong Learning. The greatest recognition, however, was reserved for the students.

Arriving as somewhat reluctant participants, they soon grew into their role as university students. They used their personalised support to produce rigorous, academic work, growing in confidence and into their 'student' role. The end result was something that few could have ever imagined when they attended the first course; a graduation ceremony. As an award of Queen Margaret University, the students graduated from the Division of Health & Health Sciences in a formal ceremony alongside students from occupational therapy, physiotherapy and the like. They received their certificates from the Chancellor of the university, often with friends and family watching on. Few could have anticipated such an achievement but now had new confidence in their skills and abilities.

Conclusion

The authors look back with joy at what was achieved; the hundreds of people who went through the programme and changed as a result of having an opportunity for self-exploration, self-acceptance and intellectual engagement with the person-centred approach. As trainers, we witnessed the transformational growth of the students. We can only guess at the subsequent impact on the lives of the people they served. However, many stories over the years suggested that relationships between care-givers and the people they served were greatly enriched, with deep levels of understanding and respect being evident.

It is also heartbreaking, knowing what is possible when the core conditions are present, to see the current lack of value being placed on the relational approach and the consequent crisis in social care in many parts of the world. Our hope is that this chapter is an indication of the importance and value of investing in the people who care as much as the people who need to be cared for.

Notes

1 Rogers, C.R., *Client Centred Therapy* (Constable, 1951)
2 Rogers (1951)
3 Adams, J.D., Hayes, J. and Hopson, B., *Transition: Understanding and Managing Personal Change* (Martin Robertson, 1976)
4 Luft, J. and Ingham, H., *The Johari window, a graphic model of interpersonal awareness*, Proceedings of the Western Training Laboratory in Group Development. Los Angeles: University of California (Los Angeles, 1955)
5 Rogers (1951)
6 Rogers (1951)
7 Berne, E., *Games People Play* (Grove Press Publications, 1964)
8 Egan, G., *The Skilled Helper* (Cengage Learning, 2001)

5 Artificial Intelligence, Technology Evolution and the Person-Centred Approach

Gareth Pierce

Artificial intelligence (AI) technology is an accelerating and often divisive force of change in all aspects of our lives, including counselling and psychotherapy. Although often thought of as a recent phenomenon, there has been an interest in machine-based counselling and psychotherapy since as far back as 1966 when ELIZA,[1] the first counselling AI, was developed to imitate the empathic communication style of Carl Rogers. Recent years have seen explosive growth in the utilisation of large language model-based AI systems such as ChatGPT[2] with a growing impact on the existing base of technology-based service provision to clients. As both a Robotics and Autonomous Systems Engineer and a fully qualified and practising person-centred counsellor, I am energised and inspired by these recent developments but understand that others question the extent to which AI can support counselling processes. Will AI be limited to background support operations, such as screening, or could it move into the counsellor's territory and start to satisfy Rogers' conditions[3] for therapeutic process?[4] Can a machine truly provide empathy, congruence and unconditional positive regard? And does it matter objectively if it does or not; would it be sufficient if the client were to perceive these needs as being met?

Most practicing counsellors, myself included, will have limited experience of using AI in their counselling practice at the moment, beyond perhaps its use for screening and supporting ChatBot style interventions. I therefore propose to discuss the wider implications for the profession, feedback from colleagues, and my personal experiences of how some of the underlying questions raised by AI relate to client experiences in relation to therapeutic alliance, empathy, unconditional positive regard and congruence.

A Brief History of AI in Counselling

Debate in psychotherapy and counselling around the uptake of AI has been evident since the demonstration in 1966 of ELIZA,[5] the first AI demonstrated in counselling which employed Natural Language Programming (NLP) designed to emulate the style of Carl Rogers. Reports of patient disclosure and engagement with ELIZA[6] were impressive, but started to raise fundamental

DOI: 10.4324/9781003536048-8

questions around ethics, confidentiality and data storage/security which persist to this day.

Progress since ELIZA has been rapid and significant. In his 2019 review of the field Fulmer[7] set out an implementation framework consisting of four levels; 1. Historical, 2. Contemporary, 3. Artificial General Intelligence and 4. Superintelligence asserting that applications in counselling are currently at level 2 (contemporary), with basic responses attained and goal accomplishment likely, but not yet meeting the requirements of empowering and establishing a professional relationship; two of the three pillars of counselling[8] described by the American Counselling Association (ACA). Luxton[9] details the development of expert systems approaches, virtual agents, therapeutic gaming, wearable technologies, mental state inference, simulation of disorders and robotics, describing how data is used in surveillance and public health research, and the ethical implications surrounding all this new technology. There is a recognition that AI could act as a super-clinician[10] using extra perception such as infra-red imaging to detect and monitor emotive responses including body temperature changes, somatic effects indicative of changes in internal states, facial expressions,[11] eye blinking, vocal characteristic and intonation, and humour.[12] Perhaps such additional data sources could help to increase the sense of relational depth perceived by the client as well as assisting a human practitioner with records review, monitoring physiological data and pre-treatment clinical interviews, thus easing demands on background work and allowing greater focus on building psychological contact.

However, despite the promise of AI, such rapid developments have raised concerns in the counselling community. As far back as 1966 Weizenbaum raised the question of to whom clients were actually disclosing. More recent studies have highlighted similar concerns,[13] therapeutically and ethically, around data security with the prevalence of Chatbots; possible bias, where human prejudices or discriminatory patterns are unintentionally, or intentionally, encoded into them; data security issues and comments on the improved memory capabilities of Chatbots over humans as well as the capacity to add supra-human measurement capability. Others have examined therapeutic alliance in AI based counselling with some commentators of the opinion that they are far from establishing therapeutic alliance with clients[14] while others have identified that difficulties can be encountered in the identification of core problems and providing individual feedback.[15]

Such concerns are real and will no doubt continue to shape the implementation of AI in counselling but, I should be clear that there is a comparatively small but growing body of evidence to support AI uptake in process-related clinical activities and the first signs of emergent capability towards more empathic interactions; it is early days at the moment, but emotive response recognition is a clear steer towards improved empathic perception.

Reflections on Practice

My experience of opinions towards AI in the counselling profession have been during numerous reflective group sessions, when generally negative sentiment was encountered towards the idea that a machine-to-human interaction could potentially offer Rogers' core conditions in a person-centred framework.[16] I was intrigued to consider some paradoxes that struck me at the time around delivery mechanisms, particularly the differences between telephone-based counselling, telemedicine approaches, including video calls, and the then accepted gold standard of face-to-face, in the room, human-to-human experience. The clinical training requirements laid out by The British Association for Counselling & Psychotherapy (BACP) at the time, 2019, mandated that the majority of counselling contact hours must be attained through the latter route; the implication being that this was in some way superior or more demanding than other delivery methods. The rise of COVID in 2020 turned this accepted wisdom on its head and suddenly video call counselling became much more widely accepted; this acceptance persisting to the present day when many organisations maintain much greater flexibility in therapy delivery. To me, this raises an interesting consideration; that the previous paradigm was rapidly overturned in the face of a disruptive event (COVID), and that it turned out that a lot of people, clients and counsellors alike, could work effectively in a different way after all.

Fulmer[17] touches on criticisms of AI in counselling, that no machine is human, and that even if a machine can emulate empathy, for example, that it would not be real empathy, and that the client would see through this chimaera. It is an emotive subject, and one that can polarise opinion. In 2020, Doraiswamy et al. surveyed 791 mental health professionals[18] of whom 17% felt future AI could provide empathic care, perhaps a surprisingly high figure. However, ultimately who determines such clinical truth for the client? If clients perceive empathy, then is that not enough? Can empathy come from non-human sources and be useful? It's clear that animal therapy[19] has long been recognised as helpful to humans in combating psychological disorders. Evidence for clients' perception of machine empathy dates back to ELIZA[20] and perhaps future technology developments in AI will increase clients' perception of receiving empathy from machines. It is likely that the skill and degree to which humans are able to encode this empathy trait, whilst mindful of the introduction of bias,[21] will ultimately determine the client experience.

For the condition of offering/receiving unconditional positive regard, many authors have commented on clients feeling less judged by a machine, and better able to disclose,[22] perhaps reminiscent of the disinhibition effect when conducting telephone counselling. Cook & Doyle[23] comment on the establishment and demonstration of the working alliance when considering online therapy in comparison to in the room, face-to-face work, concluding that working alliance is strong in both, and that disinhibition in online work can be helpful in some circumstances. The dangers around disinhibition are well understood, in that the client can disclose things at a pace beyond their capacity, in this way, the moderating operation of the room experience is preferred for some clients.[24]

The question of congruence in AI and counselling I have found, surprisingly, not to be discussed widely in the literature, perhaps because of the difficulty in understanding what we actually mean by intelligence[25] in relation to ourselves as well as machines. Tudor & Worrall[26] set out four key elements of congruence from Rogers' definition; self-awareness, self-awareness in action, communication, and appropriateness.[27] It's certainly the case that in the current state of AI, self-awareness has not been demonstrated and therefore one of the core conditions for the person-centred counselling process could not currently be met by a machine.

As part of my counselling work, I have undertaken work with many neurodivergent clients, some with a diagnosis of autism. My experience has highlighted the separation in alignment of frames of reference as described by the client and forced me to reflect on what it means to deliver an empathic response when there is large separation in frames of reference. It feels like there may be parallels in understanding the needs and processes of neurodivergent clients and how we perceive AI. Milton[28] and Singer[29] describe the neurodiversity landscape and the challenges faced by autistic individuals in being recognised and seen from their perception of reality and self. Milton describes the 'double empathy'[30] problem in interaction between individuals with different world experiences. My neurodivergent clients often comment on being challenged by feeling that others are not in their frame of reference and a sense of not being in touch with their own frame. This reminds me of the arguments around AI, whether it can be truly empathic, congruent, exhibit unconditional positive regard, etc., or whether it's just emulating these things. Interestingly it seems that for some autistic clients, robot-based interventions[31] are preferred.[32] A recent review of randomised controlled trials of robotics in psychosocial healthcare[33] concluded that although there is some positive evidence for such use of robotics in counselling, more research is needed to establish clinical outcomes.

Discussion and Conclusion

Taking a wider view of psychological support, Allen[34] estimates that worldwide 792 million people live with mental health disorders and that there are nowhere near enough mental health professionals to treat them all. Bickman[35] identifies that more than half of adults with mental illness receive no treatment and that evidence-based services are often not well implemented. So it's clear that opportunities may exist for AI systems to help address both the capacity shortage and to enable more clients to access services by reducing barriers.

Improved diagnostic systems[36] can help to target therapy more effectively and services such as Chatbots are always available to suit the time needs of the client. Crucially the AI acts to supplement existing tools, not replace them and it may be that AI applications are more geared towards counselling modalities with a structured approach, such as cognitive behavioural therapy, at least to begin with.

Ethical considerations regarding AI in counselling are likely to present a significant barrier to implementation. Luxton[37] discusses this from early considerations with ELIZA through to the recognition that emotional engagement and transference can become strong. While a desirable outcome in appropriate therapeutic settings, what happens if clients become overly attached to AI systems? There is potential for iatrogenic effects, and ethical challenges abound, especially when working with vulnerable clients where careful screening would be required for delusional or psychotic psychopathologies. Ultimately the question arises as to who is responsible for the decisions that AI makes? Allied to this are thorny questions of jurisdictional boundaries, trust, safety, confidentiality and the potential for data breaches of confidential information.

In this rich and rapidly changing AI landscape, we may ask ourselves where lies the future? Cottone[38] has argued that the current counselling paradigm, where the therapeutic relationship is constructed through a person-to-person exchange, could be shifted to a relationship with a clinical technology, with clients accessing services through electronic media, what he terms the 'techno-human' counselling paradigm.

AI technology poses some knotty problems and questions for us all. I wonder if in time, silicon or hybrid silicon/carbon-based AI technology may be accepted into the spectrum of accepted intelligence, with the recognition that AI is not fundamentally more or less, but just something different, similar to considering the spectrum of human neurodiversity. In terms of the question of whether AI can ultimately demonstrate capacity for Rogers' core conditions towards humans, for example whether humans perceive such AI empathy as real, I would suggest turning the question around and asking ourselves whether we humans will be capable of providing the core conditions towards the AI machines.

Notes

1 Weizenbaum, J., 'ELIZA – A Computer Program for the Study of Natural Language Communication between Man and Machine', in *Communications of the ACM*, 9.1 (1966) pp. 36–45

2 Rajaraman, V., 'From ELIZA to ChatGPT – History of Human Computer Conversation', in *Resonance*, 28 (2023) pp. 889–905

3 Rogers, C.R., 'The Necessary and Sufficient Conditions of Therapeutic Personality Change', in *Journal of Consulting Psychology*, 21.3 (1957) pp. 95–103

4 Sharf, R.S., 'Artificial Intelligence: Implications for the Future of Counseling', in *Journal of Counseling & Development*, 64.1 (1985) pp. 34–37

5 Weizenbaum, 'ELIZA' (1966)
6 Luxton, D.D., 'Artificial Intelligence in Psychological Practice: Current and Future Applications and Implications', in *Professional Psychology: Research and Practice*, 45.5 (2013) pp. 332–39 https://doi.org/10.1037/a0034559
7 Fulmer, R., 'Artificial Intelligence and Counseling: Four Levels of Implementation', in *Theory and Psychology*, 29.6 (2019) pp. 807–19
8 Kaplan, D.M., Tarvydas, V.M. and Gladding, S.T., '20/20: A Vision for the Future of Counseling: The New Consensus Definition of Counseling', in *Journal of Counseling and Development*, 92.3 (2014) pp. 366–72
9 Luxton, D.D., *Artificial Intelligence in Behavioral and Mental Health Care* (Academic Press, 2016)
10 Luxton, 'AI in Psychological Practice' (2013)
11 Affectiva, 'Affectiva Human Perception AI Analyzes Complex Human States' (2021) https://www.affectiva.com/
12 Ramakrishna A., et al, 'Computational Modeling of Conversational Humor in Psychotherapy', in *Proceedings of the Annual Conference of the International Speech Communication Association, INTERSPEECH, 2018*. September (2018) pp. 2344–48 https://doi.org/10.21437/Interspeech.2018-1583
13 Gamble, A., 'Artificial Intelligence and Mobile Apps for Mental Healthcare: A Social Informatics Perspective', in *Aslib Journal of Information Management*, 72.4 (2020) pp. 509–23 https://doi.org/10.1108/AJIM-11-2019-0316
14 Brown, S., 'Meet the Chatbots Doing Your Job', in *Therapy Today*, 29.5 (2018) pp. 8–11
15 Graßmann, C. and Schermuly, C.C., 'Coaching with Artificial Intelligence: Concepts and Capabilities', in *Human Resource Development Review*, 20.1 (2021) pp. 106–26 https://doi.org/10.1177/1534484320982891
16 Rogers, 'The necessary and sufficient conditions…' (1957)
17 Fulmer, R., 'Counseling with Artificial Intelligence – Counseling Today', in *Counseling Today*, Jan 16 (2018)
18 Doraiswamy, P.M., Blease, C. and Bodner, K., 'Artificial Intelligence and the Future of Psychiatry: Insights from a Global Physician Survey', in *Artificial Intelligence in Medicine*, 102.November 2019 (2020) p. 101753
19 Sack, D., 'What Therapy Animals Can Teach Us About Being Human', in *Psychology Today*, 2014
20 Fulmer, R., Joerin, A., Gentile, B., Lakerink, L. and Rauws, M., 'Using Psychological Artificial Intelligence (Tess) to Relieve Symptoms of Depression and Anxiety: Randomized Controlled Trial', in *JMIR Mental Health*, 5.4 (2018) p. e64
21 Gamble, A., 'Artificial Intelligence and Mobile Apps for Mental Healthcare: A Social Informatics Perspective', in *Aslib Journal of Information Management*, 72.4 (2020) pp. 509–23
22 Lucas, G.M., et al, 'It's Only a Computer: Virtual Humans Increase Willingness to Disclose', in *Computers in Human Behavior*, 37 (2014) pp. 94–100 https://doi.org/10.1016/j.chb.2014.04.043
23 Cook, J.E. and Doyle, C., 'Working Alliance in Online Therapy as Compared to Face-to-Face Therapy: Preliminary Results', in *Cyberpsychology and Behavior*, 5.2 (2002) pp. 95–105 https://doi.org/10.1089/109493102753770480
24 Jacobs, J., 'Seeing and Being Seen in the Experience of the Client and the Therapist', in *European Journal of Psychotherapy & Counselling*, 1.2 (1998) pp. 213–30
25 Tegmark, M., *Life 3.0 Being Human in the Age of Artificial Intelligence* (Random House, 2017)
26 Tudor, K. and Worrall, W., 'Research and Practice: Congruence Reconsidered', in *British Journal of Guidance & Counselling*, 22.2 (1994) pp. 197–206 https://doi.org/10.1080/03069889408260314
27 Rogers, C.R., *On Becoming a Person* (Constable, 1961)

28 Milton, D., 'Autistic Expertise: A Critical Reflection on the Production of Knowledge in Autism Studies', in *Autism*, 18.7 (2014) pp. 794–802 https://doi.org/10.1177/1362361314525281
29 Singer, J., 'Why Can't You Be Normal for Once in Your Life?' From a "problem with No Name" to the Emergence of a New Category of Difference', in *Disability Discourse*, ed. by Corker, M. and French, S. (McGraw-Hill Education, 1999), pp. 59–67
30 Milton, D., 'On the Ontological Status of Autism: The "Double Empathy Problem"', in *Disability & Society*, 27.6 (2012) pp. 883–87
31 Riek, L.D., 'Robotics Technology in Mental Health Care', in *Artificial Intelligence in Behavioural and Mental Health Care*, ed. by Luxton, D.D. (Academic Press, 2016) pp. 185–200.
32 Diehl, J.J. and Others, 'The Clinical Use of Robots for Individuals with Autism Spectrum Disorders: A Critical Review', in *Research in Autism Spectrum Disorders*, 6.1 (2012) 249–62 https://doi.org/10.1016/j.rasd.2011.05.006
33 Robinson, N.L., Cottier, T.V. and Kavanagh, D.J., 'Psychosocial Health Interventions by Social Robots: Systematic Review of Randomized Controlled Trials', in *Journal of Medical Internet Research*, 21.5 (2019) https://doi.org/10.2196/13203
34 Allen, S., 'Artificial Intelligence and the Future of Psychiatry', in *IEEE Pulse*, 1.3 (2020) pp. 2–6 https://doi.org/10.1109/MPULS.2020.2993657
35 Bickman, L., *Improving Mental Health Services: A 50-Year Journey from Randomized Experiments to Artificial Intelligence and Precision Mental Health, Administration and Policy in Mental Health and Mental Health Services Research* (Springer US, 2020) p. xlvii https://doi.org/10.1007/s10488-020-01065-8
36 Mody, V. and Mody, V., 'Mental Health Monitoring System using Artificial Intelligence: A Review' *IEEE 5th International Conference for Convergence in Technology (I2CT)*, Bombay, India (2019) pp. 1–6
37 Luxton, D.D., 'Recommendations for the Ethical Use and Design of Artificial Intelligent Care Providers', in *Artificial Intelligence in Medicine*, 62.1 (2014) pp. 1–10 https://doi.org/10.1016/j.artmed.2014.06.004
38 Cottone, R., 'Paradigms of Counseling and Psychotherapy, Revisited: Is Social Constructivism a Paradigm?', in *Journal of Mental Health Counseling*, 29.3 (2007) pp. 189–203 https://doi.org/10.17744/mehc.29.3.2125224257006473

6 Neurodiversity and the Person-Centred Approach

Am I Doing This Right?

Sonny Hallett

My counsellor and I meet out in the woods every week; we walk and sit on mats on the ground, notice the changing seasons in the plants, fungi and wildlife, talk or walk in silence. This time I've asked him to show me how to make a fire without a lighter. He shows me how to use the striker against the kindling, bundling twigs and strips of cloth along with a piece of King Alfred's cake, a fungus that burns very slowly. He passes the pieces over to me. 'Just have a play with it'.

I feel a familiar anxious turning-over in my stomach as I fumble the handful. I'm used to being uncoordinated, misunderstanding instructions. I often try to study how to do something on my own and practice obsessively before I let anyone watch me. It feels newly bold of me to ask someone to show me something when I haven't prepared by trying to study on my own. By practicing a skill alone, I can get a feel for it, make mistakes and try things out. I find that there is something very soothing and satisfying about this, but the process of being observed in learning and exploring can feel very vulnerable.

I realised I am autistic almost ten years ago, when in my late twenties, though I always felt that something was different. Academically I did okay because I could go away and study alone, carefully and intensively, making the most of my tendency and ability to be sucked monotropically[1] into intense interests and passions. I also did okay with art because I spent a lot of time drawing on my own, when I was anxious or to express and process my feelings. Over time, I got a lot of positive encouragement so I mostly felt confident to be seen making art. But with sports, music, learning another language or anything that required practice with other people, I felt dread. Everyone got things wrong, but I seemed to get things wrong in weird ways; somehow I felt I was even getting it wrong, wrong. People would laugh, get frustrated, be confused at why I'd come to the conclusions I did, or how I took instructions overly literally or differently from everyone else.

I think when we respond to things differently to the majority around us from when we are very small, there can be a sense of conditionality, even in the smallest interactions. The mistakes and misunderstandings I made felt so far beyond acceptable, although they were just regular mistakes and

DOI: 10.4324/9781003536048-9

misunderstandings, albeit eccentric ones, that I felt like I needed to be more, better, exceptional, to have space and safety to explore the world around me. To explore and play in art class, I needed to be extra good. For me to give voice to my weird conclusions in English and history, I needed my teachers to believe I was exceptional. Socially, I didn't have a clue where to begin, despite taking books on body language and friendship from the school library. Sometimes other kids took me under their wing and tried to show me what to wear and how to be more socially 'normal', but it felt wrong and dangerous, like I was trying to operate to too many contradictory rules that didn't make sense, and didn't even feel like me, navigating a narrow bridge over lava with no room for mistakes.

University and young adulthood gave me slightly more space to be different, and I increasingly embraced the label of weirdness, but there was always a sense that if people saw the true weirdness of my fully congruent self, I wouldn't be acceptable at all as a person – and indeed people generally didn't understand my sensory differences, my meltdowns, my intense hyperfocus, my social uncertainty. Verbal instructions were still confusing, and I still interpreted them in ways that sometimes confounded the people around me. It was only on my own in nature that I felt I could be really congruent, fully expand into the shape of myself unobserved and unobstructed. I enrolled on entomology courses, studied amphibians and reptiles, birds, plants and fungi. I kept track of all the different species of ladybird in a nearby park. Getting to know the natural spaces around me felt like the only way to feel fully at ease with myself, on my own terms – as long as I could be alone and unobserved. In nature, I couldn't get it wrong. When I got lonely, I braced myself for being around others, juggling the exhaustion of feeling constantly alert and constrained; and for the sleepless nights going over every interaction, wondering if I did the socialising wrong.

When I realised I am autistic, I discovered a whole population of people who share my experiences, many of whom have been worrying that they've been doing it wrong, or have been told as much, all their lives. I attended a support group for autistic people diagnosed in adulthood, but it was run at the time by non-autistic people and felt like it was just confirming the ways in which we were doing it all wrong, albeit through no fault of our own. I couldn't stick to it for long. However, not long after that, I spent time in autistic-led spaces – Autscape,[2] a conference run by and for autistic people, and later small groups meeting locally and online to explore and share our experiences of the world.

My first memory of Autscape was of listening to people animatedly talk about their sometimes very niche interests, feeling shared joy in their excitement and experiencing others sharing joy in my excitement. We could share our social uncertainties more openly with each other, check that we were not misunderstood or didn't misunderstand: 'I was too overwhelmed just now so couldn't concentrate on your story, but I did want to hear it – do you mind telling it again?', 'I waved at you earlier but you didn't wave back and I got into a bit of an RSD[3] spiral, but I just remembered you're face blind and maybe didn't recognise me?' or 'Would you like talking company or just sitting with you company?'. These types of checking in became normalised. It felt like the start of realising that maybe I wasn't doing anything wrong, just differently.

Back in the firemaking counselling session, I'm holding the bundle of kindling and the striker, and as I try to get the sparks to catch, I notice that I have space here to explore, that I'm not feeling as self-conscious as my body is still used to being. I am immersed in the feel of the striker, the smell of smoke, the warmth in my cupped hands. Hey! I think it smells different when the fungus catches! I don't feel worried about being seen; I feel excited to be able to share my process and discoveries. It reminds me of being in autistic space.

I believe that before I learnt about the person-centred approach (PCA) in training and practice and before I experienced it in therapy, I had already experienced it fully embodied in autistic and other neurodivergent and queer spaces. The difference is that in these spaces and communities, none of us were consciously applying any approach in our interactions towards one another. Instead, we were collectively and collaboratively working to share space through a set of principles that had emerged out of our common experiences and needs, and that I think are deeply person-centred because they have to be, to hold community while also embracing difference. I am focusing here on autism, but I am also trans and mixed race, and feel similar benefits in some of these other minority communities.

It might seem strange to compare a community of equals with a therapeutic approach, but the more I think about the six conditions, the more they seem to be reflected in my experiences of autistic space. In my first time at Autscape, for example, I felt more consistent empathy from others towards me and my ways of being in the world than I ever had in other spaces. I think a lot of this is related to the Double Empathy Problem,[4] the simple idea that people with very different experiences of the world will struggle more to understand and empathise with one another. For those of us in neurological or other minorities, this can make it hard to find situations in which the majority of those around us can easily empathise with our experiences. I also felt more unconditional warmth from others towards my weird ways of being, an unconditionality that felt expansive in its embrace of difference. So many of us have been told, 'you can't do anything wrong here', or 'there are no stupid questions', only to stumble across that invisible line anyway in normative society.

In autistic spaces, congruence feels incredibly valuable; indeed it is one of the only places many of us have been able to start experimenting with being congruent around others. I'd argue that in these communities we take turns taking on the 'therapist' role of being congruent while others are incongruent, whether that is in modelling, being able to move in ways that we need to, asking for clarification, sharing how we are experiencing a space, checking when others might be struggling or opening up the space for others to experiment and grow towards congruence. I think people often discover autistic spaces while feeling deeply incongruent, having rarely felt any belonging, safety around others, having not felt okay to be observed being themselves.

I've written and spoken in the past about the deep psychological contact that can happen in these spaces; the intense connections formed when people who neuro-normative society routinely fail to connect with, finally find welcoming and empathetic connection.[5] Spaces like Autscape, and autistic people's organisations, are generally not services, and attendees or members are not service-users, or clients. We try to support ourselves and each other, and share space and in the process we upend the often hierarchical experiences many of us have had around mental health and social care provision; that we don't know how to do it right, and we need someone else to tell us. Of course, this is rarely plain sailing, and my experience of autistic space is a privileged one, borne out of being able to access these spaces, having enough support and being lucky enough to have had overwhelmingly positive encounters. I think, very much like the core conditions of the PCA being continual processes we move towards, the holding of an autistic space is something that we in these communities are continually striving for and failing at, and achieving and failing at again. We misunderstand each other, but we also know the cost of being missed, so we try again to not miss each other the next time. We are shaped and impacted by neuro-normativity, and internalise neuro-normative ideas that could impact our warmth or empathy towards each other, but many of us have a sense of how deep the normativity can run, how much it hurts us, and just how differently individuals can experience the world, so we try and make space for that.

My communities can be messy and clumsy; I think because our attempts at welcoming, empathy, and inclusion, have emerged out of desperate need and experiences of exclusion and misunderstanding, rather than being based on specific rules that we all agree to uphold. I believe similarly that Carl Rogers arrived at his ideas around the PCA through his experience and discovery that they are what's needed to embrace a person's experience of difference and incongruence, rather than an abstract sense that they are right or nice to have.

For me in my practice as a person-centred counsellor, these struggles with internalised normative ideas and hierarchies, and the ruptures and repair that come up in autistic communities, help me to look more critically at the unexamined normativity that was embedded in my core training, in assumptions about practice, in the expectations of other therapists and concerns and uncertainties felt by my mostly neurodivergent and queer clients when engaging in therapy. Like me, so many neurodivergent people worry that they are doing therapy wrong, or are about to. So many have been told that they weren't engaging, or weren't doing it right, that we are saying too little or being too much.[6] My first ever question to my supervisor was, 'am I doing this [supervision] right?' and it has taken a very long time for me to start to trust that he might really mean it when he suggests that I can't do it wrong.

I also regularly work and connect with other neurodivergent counsellors and trainees, many of whom talk about the ways in which the PCA resonates deeply with them in its potential to embrace difference, in its focus on relationship and valuing of congruence. However, almost all of us also seem to share having struggled in our therapy training and being deprived of communities with other therapists because of these spaces' unwillingness to really embrace difference. Too many of us have felt the pressure in counselling spaces of being told to just be ourselves, only to then be told, 'Oh, no. Not like that!'.

What the autistic community has shown me, and what I've experienced as an autistic person in therapy, and then in person-centred counselling training, is that the PCA has within it an invitation to dive in deeply and intensely. The core conditions aren't a passive invitation, but a challenge to meet, welcome, be alongside and continually expand ourselves and our sensitivity towards difference. It has the potential to be as much of a challenge towards connection for each of us in the moment as it might be for every autistic person who has spent our lives trying to understand and empathise with people who are different from ourselves, to help the majority feel more at ease with our differences.

When I hear about members of my communities' experiences of counselling, including person-centred counselling, I feel that not enough of the counselling establishment understands it is failing to meet those challenges. So much training around working with people who are different, or part of minority groups, is still focused on what to do with us, rather than how to do the deep internal work that would allow people with very different experiences of the world to deeply and meaningfully connect. I want to ask my non-autistic colleagues, 'What is your relationship with neurodivergence? How have you been impacted by neuro-normativity? When did you start to suspect that you are not autistic?'.

Person-centred practitioners can learn a lot from communities that have had no choice but to exist based on person-centred principles. We live in a society that is, unfortunately, often held together through conformity, normative expectations and exclusion, and I don't think it is easy to fully embrace an approach that can so radically counter that without learning what it's like trying to exist and create community outside of those constraints.

In my practice now, I try to recreate autistic space, or more broadly neurodivergent/queer space. I keep working on being consistent and clear, trying to notice my own expectations and assumptions, and collaborate on ways to share the space and connect. Sometimes I sit on the floor with the people I work with, we share fidget toys, talk about textures, use creative analogies to explore feelings, walk around outside, welcome sidetracks and distractions, share stories from neurodivergent or queer culture, reassure whenever necessary that they're not doing it wrong. I am open about my experiences and differences and I think my starting point is the knowledge that it takes a lot of continual trying and failing to be as fully as possible in another person's frame of reference; that it can be untidy, and weird, and every single day it has the potential to change me and my understanding of possible ways of being in ways that I couldn't previously imagine. Knowing that it's hard makes every moment of connection precious, and as I write this I'm realising that that's partly why congruent connection has always been so precious to me.

Back to the firemaking, counselling session: I blow gently into the bundle in my hands, enjoying the feeling of breathing something so potentially powerful into being. Small flames flicker out of gaps between the kindling, darkening the dry wood. More than enjoying the process of making the fire, I am enjoying being able to share this moment, in feeling seen, in the way my counsellor has held and shared this space with me with warmth and connection and without obvious expectation. It feels really meaningful that a person can choose to try to create the conditions for this kind of exploration, growth, connection and holding. My communities got here because we've had to, but I think it can be really powerful when a person actively chooses to take on the continual challenge of meeting another person more than half-way. The PCA encapsulates a way to meet others on purpose; sometimes people who have never received that degree of effort to be met. Learning about the ways in which communities and individuals have needed to put great effort into connecting with each other, I believe, can help all person-centred practitioners connect more deeply with what it means to actively inhabit our approach, to meet people closer to where they are.

Notes

1 www.monotropism.org
2 https://autscape.org/
3 Dodson, W., 'How ADHD ignites rejection sensitive dysphoria', in *ADDitu*de, Feb. 7 2017. https://www.additudemag.com/rejection-sensitive-dysphoria-and-adhd/
4 Milton, D., Gurbuz, E. and López, B., 'The 'double empathy problem': Ten years on', in *Autism*, 26(8), 2022, pp. 1901–03. https://doi.org/10.1177/13623613221129123
5 https://medium.com/@sonnyhallett/intense-connections-2e0ecd1bcbb8; https://medium.com/@sonnyhallett/intensifying-connections-45d86b8a87fb
6 https://autisticmentalhealth.uk/counsellingreport

Section 3

The Person-Centred Approach in Universal Issues and Personal Trauma

7 The Person-Centred Approach and Working with Ex-convicts

Facilitating the Return

Elektra Diakolambrianou

Almost inevitably, when person-centred therapy students are being trained in the therapeutic conditions, the case of working with people who have committed crimes will come up in discussion. It is usually brought up as an example to point out how difficult it may be at times to have empathic understanding and unconditional positive regard towards the client, while at the same time, being congruent in the therapeutic relationship. Gillian Proctor describes this very accurately in her article *Working in Forensic Services in a Person-centered Way*:

> Students of PCT often ask: how can you experience unconditional positive regard (UPR) or empathic understanding for a client who has raped or murdered? How can you be congruent if you are horrified by what your client has done? How can you feel free to be yourself if you feel afraid of the client?[1]

Of course, the PCT training group where I was trained was no different. Numerous such questions arose, especially regarding unconditional positive regard, and they were usually not asked rhetorically but addressed specifically to one of our trainers: Evangelos (Vangelis) Kanavitsas. We often referred to him as the personification of unconditional positive regard, which was no coincidence given his professional background. Vangelis has been working as a psychologist at the Korydallos Correctional Facility since 2007, where he offers psychotherapeutic support to inmates, both in individual and group sessions. Moreover, he participates in the design and implementation of educational and therapeutic programmes within the prison and supervises psychology students who are doing their internship there.[2]

When faced with our questions, he would, of course, prompt us to self-reflect instead of giving us easy answers. What did unconditional positive regard mean for us? What obstacles could we identify within ourselves towards it? What did the mental construct of the hypothetical client with a criminal background look like in our minds? But sooner or later, within the

DOI: 10.4324/9781003536048-11

discussion, he would also share with us some of his personal thoughts and reflections on his experience. This 'distilled wisdom' was, for us, always valuable food for thought, usually leaving us feeling in awe and inspired but sometimes also astounding us. One such bewildering moment was when he shared with us that he never asks the inmates he works with what they are in prison for; unless they decided to share this information with him themselves, he would neither ask them about it nor try to get this information through their files. We simply could not wrap our heads around it; was he indeed working with criminals without knowing what kind of crime they had committed? 'I do not need to know that in order to do my job' was his dumbfounding answer.

The time would come for me to distill my own wisdom on the field when, in 2018, I started working at Epanodos, first as a volunteer and later as an employee. Epanodos, [επάνοδος; epánoδos] a Greek word that means return, comeback, revival, returning home after a long absence, is a public legal entity in Greece which operates under the supervision of the Ministry of Citizen Protection and aims to support ex-convicts in their social reintegration. The services provided there include psychosocial support, legal counselling, career counselling, support for essentials and housing needs, training programmes and liaising with other relevant NGOs and authorities. Contacting Epanodos is not mandatory for people being released from prison but something that is usually recommended to them by the social services of the correctional facilities; the services are offered upon request and according to an individual reintegration plan co-created by the beneficiary and the psychosocial counsellor during the first induction session. I worked there until 2022, and my duties included conducting induction sessions with new beneficiaries, providing psychological support to those requesting it, training volunteers, and supervising students who did their practicum in Epanodos. Moreover, I participated in an Erasmus+ strategic partnership project called 'Convicts Upskilling Pathways'[3] through which I offered soft skills training to participant inmates at the Correctional Facility of Halkida in Greece.

To discuss my experience from a person-centred perspective, it is important to examine the framework for offender-based counselling and its particularities. Unlike many forensic settings, including the one Gillian Proctor discusses in her previously mentioned article,[4] in Epanodos none of the beneficiaries are forced to be there. In fact, even at the prison based training programme, the inmates applied voluntarily to participate, and their applications were evaluated using criteria set by the project coordinators.[5] At the same time, their entire reintegration plan, including any therapeutic goals, was co-created with the beneficiaries and not set by the counsellors or pre-decided by the institution. This provided the ex-offenders with the opportunity to have agency and responsibility over their reintegration process, while at the same time providing the counsellors with the ability to 'be non-directive in a directive setting' as Lisbeth Sommerbeck has beautifully phrased it.[6]

One important aspect of working with ex-offenders is the transient nature of their state, and the subsequently brief therapy approach of the counselling provided to them. Most beneficiaries seek the services of Epanodos right after their release, and the post-release phase can be especially uncertain, chaotic and transitory. As they attempt to orient themselves in their new reality, both their external and internal circumstances may at any point lead them to change direction. In addition, the obstacles to reintegration can increase the chances of recidivism.[7] At the same time, Epanodos sets a limit of 12 psychological counselling sessions available per beneficiary. Although this limit is rarely strictly enforced, it aims to contribute to the process of identity reconstruction beyond the entrapping identity of the 'ex-offender'. The cornerstone of this reconstruction is the adoption of desistance – the ongoing process of leaving behind patterns of offending and criminal behaviour. Rhoden et al.[8] point out that the transformation from an offending identity into a pro-desistance identity is a deciding desistance-promoting factor, and Grommon & Rydberg[9] specifically underline the importance of such self-narratives during the immediate post-release period.

Thus, the rationale behind this particular policy of Epanodos is that by gradually referring beneficiaries to other organisations that are not-related to their ex-offender status, this process of identity transformation is catalysed. In any case, this can lead to a time-limited frame, which may not be what a person-centred counsellor is used to, but is still very effective and loyal to the PCA values because it is adapted to the reality and needs of the clients in transient states; a reality where most things are temporary and uncertain, and the person seeks ways to meet their needs despite this instability. In Keith Tudor's book on brief person-centred therapies,[10] Barrie Hopwood gave the title *This Could Be the Last Time* to his chapter on working in a young offenders' institution.[11] Although he is discussing this in the context of working with young offenders who may at any point be moved on through the system, this phrase very accurately describes the potential temporality of working with ex-offenders as well. I have to say that this experience of applying the PCA in a time-limited setting significantly expanded my understanding about the inherent adaptability, responsiveness, and deep respectfulness that characterises the PCA. And at the same time, it forever changed what the 'here-and-now' in psychotherapy means for me; after all, every here-and-now is unique and fleeting, unprecedented and irreproducible.

Another challenge of working with ex-offenders is the unavoidable necessity of learning to cope with frustration and a hardly ever easy external reality. Some of the people I worked with were homeless, facing daily adversities that ranged from hunger to being attacked by neo-Nazi organisations. Some were undocumented migrants and asylum seekers, with minimal chances of obtaining a residence and work permit. Some lacked a support network that could help them reintegrate and transform their lives; on the contrary, at times the people around them were a relapse risk. And some, unfortunately, did relapse.

At times I found it extremely hard to keep an optimistic mindset, while the external and societal circumstances constantly threatened to ruin our efforts in therapy, or not even allow them. In all honesty, I cannot say that it ever becomes easy, but what really helped me find in me the courage to cope was essentially learning to confront the social realities in the same way I encounter a client: in the here-and-now, with the therapeutic conditions and my authentic self as my only tools, and without any intent of attempting to direct the process. As Peter Schmid has beautifully phrased it 'the challenge is not to save the world but to encounter it', and to view our role as a political confrontation of reality and as 'therapy in and therapy of society'.[12] Therefore, it really became my daily mantra to keep on believing in the beneficiaries' actualising tendency against all adversities, to keep on believing in the power of non-directivity and to stop searching for positive outcomes that were often nowhere to be found: 'the task is not to raise hopes, but to facilitate hope'.[13]

Lastly, and in order to circle back to where I started in this chapter, the importance of unconditional positive regard cannot be stressed enough when working with ex-offenders. In fact, I would say that working with ex-offenders is a great way of deeply understanding the true meaning of unconditional positive regard, away from common misunderstandings of the concept; for example, confusing unconditional positive regard with agreement, validation, or approval of the client's actions and choices. After working at Epanodos, when asked to define unconditional positive regard, I reply that for me it's just regarding your client as a fellow human who, just like you, deserves to be treated with respect and dignity. Beyond what an ex-convict may have done to end up in a correctional facility, in the counselling context they are yet another client who seeks to be valued as a whole person and to have their experience seen and heard without any judgement or evaluation.[14] Yet another client who needs the therapeutic conditions in order to gradually become more aware of the implicit meanings underlying their behaviour and choices, as well as to find more authentic and socially constructive ways to express and fulfil their needs.[15] And, ultimately, yet another client who deserves to be encountered in the here-and-now, in the true existential meaning of encounter that can allow their self-healing potential to be discovered,[16] no matter what they have done in the there-and-then.

And this is why, when I was being asked by trainees and supervisees in Epanodos why I never asked a beneficiary about their criminal record unless they themselves felt it was important to mention, I always replied exactly like Vangelis Kanavitsas all those years ago; 'I do not need to know that in order to do my job'.

Notes

1 Proctor, G., 'Working in forensic services in a person-centered way' in *Person-Centered & Experiential Psychotherapies*, 4(1), 2005, pp. 20–30. https://doi.org/10.1080/14779757.2005.9688365

2 https://person-centred.gr/team/vaggelis-kanavitsas/
3 https://www.cup-project.eu/en/
4 Proctor, G., 'Working in Forensic Services' 2005
5 https://www.cup-project.eu/wp-content/uploads/CUP_Blueprint_agg_01122022.pdf
6 Sommerbeck, L., 'Being nondirective in directive settings' in *Person-Centered & Experiential Psychotherapies*, 11(3), 2012, pp.173–89.
7 https://worldpopulationreview.com/country-rankings/recidivism-rates-by-country
8 Rhoden, N., Senker, S. and Glorney, E., 'A qualitative exploration of the role of employment in desistance and subsequent identity change; ex-prisoners' lived experiences' in *Journal of Forensic Practice*, 24 (2) 2022, pp. 168–183.
9 Grommon, E. and Rydberg, J., 'Desisters in the making? Exploring the capacity to desist during community transition among a small longitudinal panel of releasees' in *Journal of Crime and Justice*, 41, 2016, pp. 1–19.
10 Tudor, K. (ed.) *Brief person-centred therapies* (SAGE Publications Ltd, 2008). https://doi.org/10.4135/9781446221297
11 Hopwood, B., 'This could be the last time: Person-centred counselling with young men in a young offenders' institution' in *Brief person-centred therapies* (SAGE Publications Ltd, 2008), pp. 148–57. https://doi.org/10.4135/9781446221297
12 Schmid, P.F., 'Person and society: Towards a person-centered sociotherapy' in *Person-Centered & Experiential Psychotherapies*, 14(3), 2015, pp. 217–35. https://doi.org/10.1080/14779757.2015.1062795
13 Schmid, P.F., 'The power of hope: Person-centered perspectives on contemporary personal and societal challenges' in *Person-Centered & Experiential Psychotherapies*, 18(2), 2019, pp. 121–38.
14 Weaver, L., 'Facilitating change in men who are violent towards women: Considering the ethics and efficacy of a person-centered approach' in *Person-Centered & Experiential Psychotherapies*, 7(3), 2008, pp. 173–84.
15 Gunst, E., 'Experiential psychotherapy with sex offenders: Experiencing as a way to change, to live more fulfilling lives, to desist from offending' in *Person-Centered & Experiential Psychotherapies*, 11(4), 2012, pp. 321–34.
16 Schmid, P.F., '"All real life is encounter" On the sustainable relevance to be surprised and affected' in *Person-Centered & Experiential Psychotherapies*, 18(3), 2019, pp. 202–13. https://doi.org/10.1080/14779757.2019.1650812

8 The Value of the Person-Centred Approach When Discussing Death and Dying

Stephanie Hutchinson

Odd as it may seem to some, I find talking about death, dying and bereavement energising. For me it's certainly more satisfying than talking about sex, possibly because the former now feels considerably more taboo than the latter. It was not ever thus. Just 100 years ago death was more common, more visible and more likely to be played out in the family or community domain. However, remarkable advancements in medical interventions have occurred in the past century, helping people live a lot longer, in the Western world at least, and there is a sense that life should be prolonged at all costs. Thus, the experience of dying can be medicalised and narrow in focus with a consequence being the development of a 'death denial' attitude within modern, Western society. This, coupled with the fact that the post-dying processes tend towards formulaic and often profit driven, means the dying and the bereaved are negatively impacted on many levels: emotionally, spiritually, financially.

I know this, not just because I've studied it and witnessed it in my role as a grief counsellor at a hospice, but because I have experienced it. My own fairly early bereavements, orphaned at 28 is my wry way of describing it, gave me an insight into how marginalised the grief experience can be for many. Even at the time though, I refused to be cowed by people's discomfort and would not avoid the topic of my parents' deaths; perhaps instinctively taking a person-centred stance and valuing my own needs and experience over societal norms. Indeed, it may even be fair to say that I relished talking about death in an almost anarchic, punk kind of way, shaking my fist at the Western establishment and saying 'come on, who are you kidding? It's an unavoidable part of the human experience so let's get in there and talk about it! No more deathly silences. Let's break that taboo'.

And perhaps these days taboo is too strong a word – I hope so. I hope instead that people's reluctance to enter that conversational arena is more an individual reticence than a social constraint, related to a fear of saying the wrong thing rather than believing 'one doesn't speak of such things'. Certainly, my 'punk' attitude could now be considered much more 'establishment'

DOI: 10.4324/9781003536048-12

given that in 2022 the eminent medical journal *The Lancet* released the report of their Commission on the Value of Death,[1]

> Death, dying, and grieving today have become unbalanced. Health care is now the context in which many encounter death and as families and communities have been pushed to the margins, their familiarity and confidence in supporting death, dying, and grieving has diminished. Relationships and networks are being replaced by professionals and protocols.

The report sets out five principles, ideally underpinning a new vision of how death and dying could be. Another heartening development is the concept of Compassionate Communities, which is becoming core to many Western countries' public health approaches to palliative care. Originating in Australia almost 25 years ago, the term 'describe(s) communities which play a much stronger role in the care of people at end of life and their families and carers through illness, dying, death and bereavement'.[2]

These developments I believe can be tied to the ripple effect of the person-centred approach (PCA) which seeks to understand both individual and collective experience and appreciates the value of human relationality. However, there is still a fair way to go. My work focuses on empowering people to make more informed decisions about what their dying, their funerals, their legacy might look like. I present seminars that aim to normalise speaking about dying, about death, about grief and loss and I firmly believe that my training in the PCA has made me a far better facilitator of this work than I might otherwise have been; raging against the machine can only take one so far after all!

A Personal View of Death and Dying

In New Zealand the Māori culture has the ritual of pepeha[3] when new people gather together, a way of introducing yourself in Māori. It tells people who you are by sharing your connections with the people and places that are important to you and the people you are connected to. At the very first seminar, I share what I call my 'death pepeha'; my connection and my experiences of death. It feels important to do this, to offer my 'why' in terms of doing the work, to own my story, to set out my frame of reference.

Participants will learn that my mother died first and that her funeral was awful. It took place on my 20th birthday, however, that was very much by the by. I think the main source of the event's bleakness was that my father had listened to his father when he said 'in these circumstances, you have a private, family funeral'. The 'circumstances' were that after many years of ill mental health, my mother took her life. So it was, on a grey, slightly rainy day in September that 12 family members gathered around the graveside to listen to a minister fumble his way through a very short and wholly inadequate overview of my mother's life.

My father's funeral took place eight and a half years later. He died of cancer so a more socially acceptable death! By then, my siblings and I were able to act, in PCA terms, according to an internal locus of evaluation rather than an external one and thus make decisions less constrained by any perceived social conventions. We originally thought we would have the service at the funeral home as he wasn't religious. However, once having sighted it, in all its red, velvet, incongruous, plush glory, we changed our minds and even though the notice had been published, instead found a modern high vaulted church with exposed beams that felt more appropriate given our father worked with wood. I chose to deliver one of the eulogies and we children carried the coffin from the church. Perhaps not particularly unusual now, 32 years ago it was.

I brought these experiences to my training in the PCA and even then could see that there were far wider applications of the approach than merely in the therapy room. It is very much a way of being, and I personally see it as a philosophical approach to life, and as an imperfect and very much on-going practice! As well as Carl Rogers' writings and research, I have also been influenced by author and research professor Dr Brené Brown's work on shame and vulnerability, worthiness and belonging.[4] My training both in the PCA and in the work of Dr Brown have definitely contributed to how I'm now able to perceive and process attitudes around dying, death and bereavement and also how I challenge them and attempt to broaden the discourse in the realm of what is, these days, described as 'death literacy'.

Death Literacy

I wasn't aware of the phrase 'death literacy' when developing my 'No More Deathly Silences' workshops in Scotland, only hearing it back in my native New Zealand. It's useful in articulating the guiding principle of my experiential, psycho-socio-educative 'Dying Matters' workshops; raising the levels of literacy by providing opportunities for people to explore and express their experiences of dying, death and bereavement, and discover information and insights that might empower them to continue conversations with their families, communities, and networks.

I think it would be fair to say that in attempting to raise levels of death literacy, I'm also working with levels of emotional literacy which can seem a gargantuan task so I'm grateful for my experience of, and training in, person-centred facilitation. Rogers' Fundamentals of a Center for Person-Centered Learning[5] are an important reference point. Although he was referring to more traditional educational environments such as schools, colleges, universities or graduate schools, I feel Rogers identifies important elements that are conducive to any collective learning situation and most definitely contribute to the vibe I wish to create in my workshops.

Rogers describes how, as a precondition for learning, I need to be sufficiently secure within myself and my relationship to others to be able to trust the participants to share the responsibility for their own learning. By offering them the core conditions, I create a safe space within which participants are able to share their experience, prior learning, and knowledge. Thus, they can learn from each other and shape their own learning.[6] Specifically the precondition speaks to me about the practice of humility, a value of mine identified via Brené Brown's work, and not hiding behind any perceived role or expertise, instead, as per the PCA, remaining open to the experience of others. So, although I currently work for a hospice and offer my workshops in that capacity, I do my best to be clear that the information I share is not the holy grail of knowledge, rather a collection of ideas to be discussed and tried on for size. And it is definitely via participants' sharing that much is learned and gained, in the talking that so much happens for people. As I say to participants: we often describe conversations about death and dying as 'difficult or hard conversations' when perhaps it is simply that they are unfamiliar conversations.

As facilitator in this space, I want to respect and respond to what might organically arise amongst participants so while I have my information and points of discussion lined up, I try to remain fluid and flexible and non-directive rather than try to strictly adhere to a game plan. Indeed, I have recently rebranded from offering Dying Matters 'workshops' to offering Dying Matters 'seminars' after learning that 'seminar' comes from the Latin seminarium which means plant nursery or seed plot. It not only sounds more sophisticated, it also feels more rich with possibility of growth – if the conditions are right, of course!

Applying the PCA to the Challenges in Talking about Death and Dying

One challenge I face is that people can come with the expectation that they will learn 'what to do' or more often 'what to say' to a grieving person. 'What is the right thing to say?' is a common question. Now, I definitely have within me a part that loves to impress with sage advice, enjoys having the answers and purrs in response to praise so let's be clear that humility is definitely an aspirational practice. Instead of advice, I offer acknowledgement of the very human desire to get it right while suggesting there is no one right answer because what might be helpful for one person, may not be helpful for another. That is what I consider to be one of the epiphanies of my person-centred training: the recognition that 'what's true for me may not be true for others'.[7] It was, for me, a very freeing philosophical tenet to grasp; the recognition and acceptance that we can all have different experiences and beliefs and no one's is more valid than anyone else's. I share that concept consistently throughout the seminars as a pathway to a broader acceptance of, for example, what a 'good funeral' might be.

I also do my best to meet people within their frame of reference with Rogers' unconditional positive regard (UPR). While I may not agree with someone's position on the important elements of a 'good funeral' for example, I absolutely respect their right to their opinion. I recognise in myself there are times when I find comfort and a sense of safety in certainty, and therefore I do empathise with people who choose a very traditional funeral because it can seem like the right/familiar/easy thing to do. However, I am a huge advocate for providing the information, the space and the permission to ponder, particularly in an increasingly secular world, what rituals and services may be an apt honouring of a life.

I appreciate that we are all shaped by our experiences, our cultures and our social conditioning and aim to demonstrate that when I am reflecting back someone's sharing. I also endeavour to help people understand the shape of their own beliefs by encouraging them to reflect on such things as their first significant bereavement and the level of support they did or did not get, what 'dying well' might look like for them, a funeral that they considered memorable and why, etc.

UPR is most definitely my mantra when it comes to the challenging discussions around embalming, with empathy, authenticity and non-directivity close behind. In New Zealand, it is estimated that between 80 and 90% of deceased are embalmed. It is not at all necessary, however, people are led to believe it is and are often unaware of more natural care processes of the dead. It is not for me to say 'it's wrong', however, I can share that, for me, the environment is important and that my learning now has me leaning towards a natural burial where embalming is not possible. And as with any discussion, I welcome all points of view. Sometimes it's difficult because there's a part of me that feels that some of the viewpoints are forged by social and capitalist conditioning and need challenging. However, I also know that accepting people where they are at is going to provide an environment much more conducive to change. Judgement can shut people down and UPR can open minds up.

One key element that helps me demonstrate that I value everyone's experience equally is the adoption of the word AND instead of BUT. We were told at primary school that 'but' is one of the joining words that connects two parts of a sentence. However, I'm of the opinion that it splits more than joins, drives disconnect rather than acceptance. Using AND can allow very different ideas and preferences to sit alongside one another with equal acceptance, not negating or diminishing one concept over another. For example, 'After death Anna would like her family to wash her body and prepare her for burial but Betty feels she couldn't place that burden on her children so wants to be taken away and embalmed'. The BUT can seem to favour the second point of view. An AND gives both equal validity. It may seem minor semantics to some, however, for me small words = big difference. And it certainly keeps me grounded in curiosity and openness, receiving everyone's input with equanimity and non-judgement. My hope is that others might then offer the same.

Applying the PCA to My Own Growth

Given the sensitive, or at least unfamiliar, subject matter and my own lived experience, I don't always manage to be the paradigm of person-centredness that I would like to be and that's also useful, at least if I can catch myself in the moment and own my gaffe or my bias. And, of course, I must remember to offer myself unconditional positive *self*-regard (UPSR). Perhaps Brown best describes the idea of UPSR with one of her 'ten guideposts to wholehearted living: Letting go of Perfectionism and Cultivating Self-Compassion'.[8] This has been important to my growth as a facilitator and feeling secure in myself as I have to practice what I preach by demonstrating self-compassion when something goes wrong. Another guidepost which serves me well in my seminars is 'Letting go of what others think and Cultivating Authenticity'[9] which speaks to Rogers' practicing of congruence or genuineness. Keeping it real means being honest about my own experience and it is only fair that if I'm inviting participants to reflect and share, then so too must I.

Thus I share that while most of the reactions or responses I experienced in my bereavements were not that helpful and some surprisingly insensitive, over the years I have actually come to the realisation that some people may well have walked away from their encounter with me kicking themselves for what they said. I now aim for UPR, or to use Brown's articulation of the concept, 'to have the most generous interpretation possible of someone's actions or words and have the attitude/belief that people are doing the best they can'.[10]

Conclusion

In many ways, I have to thank the person who said to myself and my sister in the street some months after our mother's funeral 'I'm sorry to hear your mother died but she was away a lot anyway wasn't she?'. This response has certainly been part of my motivation for providing opportunities for open and frank discussions around the big D. And whereas once upon a time I was interested in converting people to my own frame of reference, my embracing of the person-centred approach has expanded my perspective and strengthened my sense of self. My seminars are offered as a means of cultivating compassionate community initiatives; sowing seeds, sparking imaginations and hoping that something takes root and takes on a life of its own.

Knowing what I know now, I can view the experiences I had around my parents' deaths with a more generous lens and still have a passion for challenging the status quo! Death may be a universally unavoidable, at least currently, fact, however, just as every human being has their own unique experience of life, so too may they have their unique experience of death and grief and be supported in that.

Notes

1 The Lancet, *Commission on the Value of Death: Bringing Death Back into Life* (2022). https://www.thelancet.com/commissions/value-of-death
2 Compassionate Communities. https://compassionatecommunities.au/
3 https://pepeha.nz/
4 Brown, B., *The Gifts of Imperfection* (Penguin Random House, 2020)
5 Rogers, C.R., *A Way of Being* (Houghton Mifflin, 1980)
6 Rogers, C.R. (1980)
7 Sanders, P. (ed), *The Tribes of the Person-Centred Nation* (PCCS Books, 2004)
8 Brown, B. (2020)
9 Brown, B. (2020)
10 Brown, B., *Rising Strong* (Penguin Random House, 2015)

9 The Person-Centred Approach Working with Relationships

Working Therapeutically on the Cliff Edge

Jacquelyn Pratt

My introduction to relationship therapy was an awful, personal experience. It was judgemental, diminishing, divisive, generic and compelled me to want to offer something both different and better, something person-centred. Over the years, I have come to realise that there is an immense societal importance to this work. Relationships underpin everything we do from the cradle to the grave. Home, family, education, work and leisure all include the impact of relationships, both positively and negatively. A relationship can be the difference between functioning in potentiality or in deficit. How well do you function when you feel troubled by your relationship with a partner, relative, friend or work colleague? Our ability to navigate relationships determines the survival of the human species but to do that, we must cultivate resilience in surviving hurt, sometimes accept the unacceptable, accompany each other in difference and collaborate in the caretaking and nourishing of our connection.

As a person-centred practitioner I felt confident in the person-centred approach (PCA) as a collaborative process between client and therapist but had to learn how to facilitate relationship therapy; creating the conditions for relationship growth by collaboration with the individuals within a non-directive environment, offering both partners the opportunity to explore their experience of their relationship with me in a non-judgemental, validating, empathic way and for me to help them do that for and with each other. The couples provide the direction and I immerse myself to facilitate their process.

The Fundamentals of Person-Centred Relationship Therapy

Welcome to my person-centred, couple therapy consultation room. We are not alone, Peter and Lisa are sitting on the sofa together and I am sitting opposite them in my armchair, a rug between us. It is more crowded in here than it first appears. There are five relationships in the room, I with Peter, I

DOI: 10.4324/9781003536048-13

with Lisa, both with each other, I with their relationship and my relationship with myself. The second of the six necessary and sufficient conditions of person-centred therapeutic change[1] is present; Peter, Lisa and their relationship are incongruous. They are vulnerable and anxious. I can see it, there are sighs and nerves and the look I have come to recognise as the walk of shame into relationship therapy; confirmation of failure to navigate relationship without help. It is my responsibility to cultivate and facilitate therapeutic process, encompassing the remaining necessary and sufficient conditions; I'm congruent with them and myself, I have unconditional positive regard (UPR) for them and their relationship, certainly more than they currently have for each other and their relationship, and I know how hard it was for them to make their appointment and walk through my door. I still need to establish psychological contact with them, to empathically understand them and their frame of reference, to be able to experience and communicate with them with UPR and empathically informed congruence.

Before we meet Peter and Lisa more intimately, it might be helpful for you to understand the fundamentals that I believe are the foundations necessary for me to be able to facilitate the therapeutic process. They are experiential; I learned them all from the couples I've had the privilege of accompanying and they ground me as I meet the challenges couples bring. Couples need to feel I have confidence in what I am doing, otherwise it is not a safe space for them; my confidence is rooted in my foundations.

My Person-Centred Couple Therapist Foundations

First, and most importantly, I am person-centred; it feels important for me to state that. I learned the fundamentals of how to be it 20 odd years ago and I have honed my person-centred self experientially, personally and professionally over the years. It organically informs how I experience everything; it is a blessing, a hard master and a challenge. Concurrently, I am logical, pragmatic, creative, compassionate and active, assertive and challenging. You need lots of awareness to be congruent with yourself and accurate intuition to connect with people and their relationship. I work very hard, very quickly; relationship problems are on a cliff edge, there is only one last chance saloon!

It is essential to be non-judgemental of both the individuals and the relationship. I'm often asked by couples if I think they are fixable. I will tell you what I tell them – I gave up guessing years ago. I believe in the process and the outcome is whatever they choose it to be. Any bias I have, whether for or against, can only have a negative impact as I will have hijacked their process and our work will never be authentically theirs. Prizing the individuals and the relationship as an entity is essential. There is always something to value in who they are and their story that they really need to hear to be reminded that they have resources.

Empathy necessitates me performing internal and external inquiring athletics to gain understanding of the individuals and the impact they have on each other and their relationship. Building and sharing the elements of understanding with the individuals and the impact on the relationship increases awareness and helps the couple have increasing agency over themselves and their relationship.

How I experience the couple can be very impactful. I will reflect this if it feels confidently and consciously purposeful, especially if it feels more uncomfortable not to. It is only congruent if it concurrently includes empathy and UPR. A unique aspect of sharing congruence in couple work is the duality; congruence shared with an individual will concurrently be received by the other and may have an impact on the relationship with me and each other.

Person-centred therapy is a non-directive approach. I share what I believe and understand with my clients in the art of not knowing.[2] I cannot make them do anything but I cannot help them if I knowingly withhold what I have learned. I try to cultivate a relationship with them through actions, attitudes and demeanour that maximises the opportunity to facilitate their agency of themselves and their relationship.[3]

My Fundamental Beliefs about Relationships

Through the application of the PCA over many years, I've come to identify my fundamental beliefs of relationship. Brace yourself!

Love includes hurt. Love is a strong, delicious primary emotion, it therefore hurts profoundly when hurting is part of loving. This flies in the face of our societal pursuit of happiness. Meeting 'the one', 'our soulmate' is rarely caveated with 'of course you are going to hurt each other along the way'.

Whilst I have my bubble burster out – it hurts to be hurt; it also hurts to be the hurter. At the same time as no one thinks they are going to be hurt in a loving relationship, neither does anyone believe that they will be the hurter. Both experiences challenge our relationship beliefs, our self-concept and self-esteem. If I want to be with the person that hurt me, am I weak? If I hurt the person I love, do I still deserve love? All betrayal hurts but never in a linear way.

Maintain brace position – everyone is capable of betrayal, be it a broken promise, commitment, agreement or an infidelity. After accompanying so many couples and hearing so many unique stories, I can only conclude that any betrayal in a relationship arrives because of a set of circumstances where if any one of the impacting factors had been different, the event or events may never have occurred. Sliding doors and perfect storms come to mind. Most relationships have vulnerabilities, they are navigable if known and dangerous if unknown. Unknown vulnerabilities and lack of communication can produce secrets. Secrets hold hurt that is hidden but that doesn't mean that the hurt doesn't exist, it is just unacknowledged to self and unknown to the other. The hurter is responsible for the relationship injury and the hurt experienced but the relationship recovery belongs to both the hurter and the hurt.

Next, couple issues may have a familiarity and repetitiveness about them but every couple is unique. The impact of couple unhappiness and resolution or dissolution is specific to the two individual human beings and the distinctive mix that is their relationship. And a relationship is a unique, sometimes delicious and sometimes poisonous mix of loving and living. The therapeutic process clarifies for the clients, as individuals, the importance of the elements of loving and living for them and whether they can achieve those elements to their satisfaction within their relationship.

Finally, we are all caretakers of our relationships. We have 100% responsibility for our 50%. Relationships need a working relationship template, active participation and caretaking by both equally and at times compensatory. Every relationship is underpinned by a relationship agreement but too often the relationship agreement is implied or assumed. I encourage my couples to have a liveable, articulated agreement within their relationship template, especially if their relationship includes recovery from an injury. A working relationship template includes both nourishment and work-in-progress and is navigated and facilitated by good communication and action. Good communication includes both hearing and listening. Action includes invitation and acceptance of invitation to nourish and caretake the relationship.

Couple Counselling in Action: Peter & Lisa

I start every initial consultation in the same way. I ask for a potted history of their relationship, significant moments or events for themselves and what they believe are such for the other. I explain that I need to hear from both so that I can try to understand all that is going on, what's bringing them to counselling and what they would like help with. This is me beginning the process of gaining understanding, empathy and UPR for them and their relationship so that I can make psychological contact.

Peter and Lisa have been together for 16 years and married for three. They got together in their teens. It has been a tumultuous relationship, and at various points throughout the years, they've both questioned whether they should be with each other. For Peter, he fully committed to the relationship six years ago after he was unfaithful, realised it was a terrible mistake and that he never wanted to be unsure of or apart from Lisa again. Lisa knew about the betrayal, was terribly hurt but accepted the pain, and she too decided to move forward with the relationship.

They have both had career changes since then. Peter considered his career change to have nourished the relationship but Lisa's to have had a negative impact. Lisa applied and accepted her new position despite Peter's objections to both the shift patterns and the risky nature of the work. Peter believed this was outwith their relationship agreement. Lisa's new job caused the couple to spend less time together and when they did, it was spent with friends or family at group events. Both reduced their communication with each other as resentment built up on both sides. Peter did not want to hear about Lisa's work and Lisa felt resentful about that. Lisa began to share her day with work colleagues via messaging apps, with the content becoming flirty and sexual. Peter looked at her phone one night after another in a repetitive series of spiteful arguments where Lisa questioned whether she wanted to be in the marriage anymore and Peter, though equally unhappy in the relationship, was outraged that she would give up on the marriage. He was married for life!

As flies on the wall of my consulting room observing Peter and Lisa you see he is very hurt and extremely anxious, torn between being furious and fighting with himself not to break down. I congruently reflect this to him and validate his feelings. Lisa is very anxious too, sitting on the edge of the seat and seems scared to speak. When she does, Peter disagrees with her perspective, she puts her head down and silences herself. I reflect this and communicate my understanding. I share with them what I experience of their relationship. A nourishing relationship that suffered when there was lack of focused time and attention on each other and little or no communication about the relationship and the individuals in it. This absence caused unacknowledged vulnerability which neither of them was caretaking because they were unaware of self and the other, caught up in their own perspective of feeling unloved, uncared for and unappreciated. I offer an explanation of a relationship template of nourishment and work-in progress. I identify that Peter needs Lisa to caretake her half of the relationship without having to check in with him where the boundary should be and that Lisa needs Peter to know that she needs him to be interested in her and caretake his half of the relationship; that they are not just married forever, no matter how the relationship feels. We talk about what nourishment in the relationship looks and feels like and agree the work-in progress. At the end of the session Peter throws his head back and his arms in the air and says, 'Thank God, I have hope', promptly bursting into tears of relief. I believe I have confirmation I've made psychological contact.

Facilitating Resilience and Growth

At the next appointment, they start by telling me they are not sure how I did it but they both felt really understood, a clear statement that empathic reflections and validations had resonated and they experienced psychological contact. They have spent time together, alone and socially and they feel much more able to navigate this injury to the relationship. Lisa confirms taking responsibility for the relationship injury and asks for my and Peter's help for her part of the recovery. He confirms that he understands that he has a part in the recovery too. They both confirm that they appreciate the relationship template idea and caretaking responsibilities. We concentrate on communication. I model and then support them to use Caretaking Feelings Communication,[4] a development of person-centred active listening.[5] The skills of active listening include hearing and repeating back what you have heard and clarifying in pursuit of understanding. Caretaking Feelings Communication also non-judgmentally validates feelings; much time and distress can be experienced in a relationship wrestling with judging whether feelings are valid. If someone feels sad, communicates their sadness and that is validated, that is nourishing. If you have to fight for your right to be sad, it is distressing. Feelings validated and understood present the opportunity to soothe.

It generally takes a few sessions to embed this communication style as it is hard to learn to respond and not react to what you are hearing. As a listener, we often react to what we are hearing and miss the chance to confirm what we have heard, to understand and to validate. Often that's enough for soothing to occur, but further soothing could include taking responsibility for all or part, apologising, or explaining intention or misunderstanding. We cannot change what has happened in the relationship but we can change how we feel about it. I believe caretaking each others' feelings is an essential skill in creating a collaborative relationship, where both individuals in the couple can be heard and understood.

Conflict resolution is also a collaborative pursuit. Two different experiences of the same event can sit alongside each other, there does not need to be one truth overriding the other, creating this space in your relationship is immensely connecting.

As work progresses, there is often a setback. When communication and the experience of the relationship feel better, the wish list often increases and couples get bolder about what they want to achieve. This happened with Lisa, she wanted to be sure that they were both committed to being active in the relationship. It would take two more appointments before Peter's anxiety about this would be voiced. He had heard that unless he was the perfect husband and she was happy, then she would leave him. We had to work through this hidden vulnerability. Lisa was able to validate how Peter was feeling and immediately reassure him. The most difficult part for me was how to help Lisa navigate her own boundaries through the lens of caretaking the relationship. I had to be careful that Lisa concurrently experienced my congruence, empathy and UPR to facilitate her agency over herself and cultivate much needed security for Peter.

Living a Resilient Relationship

Peter and Lisa are both re-invested in their relationship. They work from a known loving and living foundation; their relationship template facilitates their identified nourishment and accepted work-in-progress and their relationship agreement is tangible, not assumed. They use a caretaking feelings communication style that both nourish them as individuals and facilitates them working through new challenges that require resilience and growth. They no longer see counselling and our relationship as a sign of failure but as a resource, they can return to because they need it, or just because they want to.

Conclusion

I believe there is a beautiful synchronicity between the PCA and working with couples, it's cultivating a therapeutic relationship with two people in relationship and with their relationship: being in relationship with relationships. When the person-centred approach is experienced and absorbed there is change and growth; you know a fundamental change has occurred when you experience a couple being person-centred to each other… and I am redundant!

Notes

1 Rogers, C.R., 'The Necessary and Sufficient Conditions of Therapeutic Personality Change', in *Journal of Counselling Psychology*, 21, pp. 5–103 (1957)

2 Bozarth, J., '"Nondirectivity" in the Theory of Carl R. Rogers: An Unprecedented Premise', in *Person-Centred & Experiential Psychotherapies*, 11 (4), pp. 262–76 (2012)

3 Schmid, P.F., 'Facilitative Responsiveness: Non-Directiveness from Anthropological, Epistemological and Ethical Perspectives', in Levitt, B. (ed) *Embracing Non-Directivity: Reassessing Person-Centred Theory and Practice in the 21st Century* (PCCS Books, 2005)

4 Pratt, J., *Caretaking Feelings Conversations Template, Glasgow Couple Counselling* (2021)

5 Rogers, C.R. and Farson, R.E., 'Active Listening' in Newman, R.G., Danzinger, M.A., Cohen, M. (eds) *Communicating in Business Today* (D.C. Heath & Company, 1987)

10 Let's Talk about Baby Loss

A Person-Centred Approach to 'Being Alongside' Bereaved Parents

Jen Keppie

Baby loss is both one of the most profound losses that someone can experience but also, paradoxically, one of the most hidden and silenced in our society. The scale of this appalling loss causes us to look away or to clumsily intervene as we struggle to know how to help. Understandable perhaps, but the impact on the grieving parents can only serve to compound their grief, despair and isolation. I am not a bereaved parent, and therefore I do not write here as a person who has experienced the loss of a baby, nor do I offer myself as an 'expert' on baby loss. I write as a person-centred counsellor who has, over a period of several years, sat with, talked to, and been alongside many bereaved parents in the aftermath of their loss or losses. What I share here is some of what I have learned from those experiences and why I believe that the person-centred approach (PCA) is a uniquely powerful 'way of being' alongside bereaved parents.

What is Baby Loss?

I would like first to define what is meant by the term 'baby loss', for reasons of clarity, but also as a means of demonstrating the diversity of experience, and the importance of language in understanding baby loss. For many of us when we hear the term 'baby loss' we perhaps think about 'miscarriage'. Miscarriage, which technically refers to all losses where a baby dies before birth and prior to 24 weeks gestation, is not a word I find helpful however, as it bundles together some vastly differing experiences whilst also failing to properly acknowledge other forms of baby loss. Instead, the terms I use are:

- early loss – typically considered under 12 weeks gestation
- second-trimester or mid-term loss – when a baby dies before birth, between 12 and 24 weeks of pregnancy
- termination for medical reasons (TFMR) – when a baby dies as a result of the pregnancy being ended by medical intervention due to a life-limiting or un-survivable medical condition

DOI: 10.4324/9781003536048-14

- stillbirth – when a baby dies before birth after 24 weeks of pregnancy
- neonatal death – when a baby is born living, even briefly, who then dies within 28 days of birth
- infant loss – when a baby dies after 28 days but before 1 year of age, with a known cause
- sudden unexpected death in infancy (SUDI) – the death of a previously healthy infant under 1 year of age, with no obvious cause

The exact definitions and terminology will perhaps vary slightly from place to place, but this is how we understand different types of baby loss in Scotland. Understanding the type of loss does not tell us everything we need to know about an individual experience, but it gives us a starting point.

The Experience of Baby Loss for the Parent(s)

When I am with a person who has experienced the loss of a baby there are two key things that I am consistently aware of. First of all, there is the uniqueness of the experience. There are some broad issues that frequently present in counselling with bereaved parents, but the full picture of loss and grief is notably unique to the individual. The type of loss, the specific circumstances of the loss, the pre-existing and on-going support network and social dynamic of the bereaved parent as well as their personal context and history all play a role in how the loss and grief is experienced and expressed.

Second, there is the societal response the bereaved parents are met with. Some, of course, are wonderfully supported by family, friends, work colleagues in the aftermath of their loss and feel well held by the care, compassion and understanding around them. It's important to acknowledge that many of these other people in the baby's life – siblings, grandparents, aunties, uncles, cousins, friends – are grieving too. My counselling practice however, and therefore the focus of this piece, centres around the experience of the parents. And the reality is that many find that their loss and the associated feelings and experiences are widely misunderstood and/or not talked about; a societal silence around the death of their baby. The experience of many bereaved parents is that people, for a multitude of reasons, don't want to, know how to, or feel able to talk about the death of a baby, the grief of the parents, or the baby that has died. And if they do, it's often not in the way that the bereaved parents need and want to talk about their experiences.

A Person-Centred Approach to Baby Loss

My way of working with clients is resolutely person-centred. I have experienced the PCA from a variety of angles, client, student, supervisee, counsellor, 'just a person' going about my day, and I consistently find it to be an eminently humane, respectful and compassionate way of being. Here, I aim to share some of my experiences of working in a person-centred way with bereaved parents and how this has been received.

First up, I would like to talk about non-directivity, as it underpins everything that I do, say, think and am in my work with bereaved parents. Some clarity about what I understand by the concept of non-directivity; I view it as an attitude of deep respect for the personhood of the other, and the endeavour not to 'get in the way' of the client's process, not to offer my own perspective uninvited, or to impose my own hopes or expectations for the client. My understanding of non-directivity could not be further from the caricatures of passivity, disinterest or kindly detachment; the 'nodding dog' stereotype. Nor do I view it as a paternalistic tool, 'I think it's best for you if you work it out for yourself'. With growing personal understanding of the concept, I have experienced a freeing, a loosening, a deeper authenticity in my way of being with clients; the understanding that it is far more about the intention and attitude with which I offer myself to the client rather than about any specific thing I say or do. I am no longer so constricted by the fear of 'am I being directive?', but instead have found more spontaneity, the ability to be more present, to offer more of myself. It seems that my deepening understanding of and capacity for a non-directive attitude has evolved in tandem with my sense of congruence, each supporting the growth of the other.

So how and why is non-directivity important in working with baby loss? Well, bereaved parents often have a lot imposed on them by others, whether it's silence, or judgement, expectations, pressure, perceptions, timelines, ideas about what grieving a baby should look like. The PCA, with its overarching principle of non-directivity, serves to counter some of the less helpful responses that bereaved parents are often met with; an antidote, if you will, to the silence and typical societal responses around baby loss. Here I'd like to look at a few ways that I can exemplify this.

Frequently Dismissed Feelings

Bereaved parents often talk about feelings of shame, self-blame, guilt, failure; wondering if they could have done more for their baby, feeling that they failed to keep their baby safe, of guilt about making the decision for TFMR, or fears that they have let their partner down by not being able to have a living child. Often these kinds of feelings are quickly shut down when a bereaved parent attempts to express them. They are told 'of course it's not your fault, you mustn't feel that way, you're not a failure'. Often well-intentioned, but these responses serve to dismiss those feelings and give the message that it's not ok to feel them or talk about them. But, of course, telling someone 'it's not your fault' doesn't make that feeling go away, so the upshot is that the bereaved parent continues to carry these, often very difficult and painful, feelings alone.

Conversely, the person-centred response is one of empathy and unconditional positive regard (UPR). It allows us to make room for these feelings, to really hear the parent and the wholeness of their experience, we don't shut down or dismiss. Consequently, the parent is no longer alone with these feelings, they have someone they can share them with, somewhere to process what it's like to carry them. From a non-directive stance, I don't seek to actively dismantle feelings such as shame or guilt. Instead, through my attitude and way of being, I offer the bereaved parent UPR and acceptance at a time they cannot offer it to themselves. This conveys, through attitude rather than explicit words, acceptance of both the feeling, 'it's ok to feel that way and talk about that stuff here', and also the person, 'I accept and value you just as you are, even whilst you believe you are a bad/unworthy/disappointing person'.

Feeling That People Don't Understand

The phrase I hear time and again from bereaved parents is 'people just don't get it'. I see this demonstrated in different ways; insensitive remarks, the implied assumption that a new baby 'makes it better', family failing to talk about the baby because 'they don't want to upset me, do they think I have forgotten my baby has died, and that mentioning her will remind me?'. It comes up in a myriad of ways, sometimes quite shocking; asking for maternity clothes because 'you won't be needing them now' or likening the loss to the death of a pet (yes, these are real examples). Other reactions simply suggest a general lack of awareness: not realising that the big milestones are often really tough, reacting awkwardly when the bereaved parent talks about or shares pictures of their baby, not understanding that you don't 'get over' the death of a baby but perhaps rather learn to 'live with' the grief in your own way and in your own time. None of these examples are intended to denigrate or shame anyone – it can be incredibly hard to know what to say, how to respond, how to be around someone whose baby has died. But rather, they are here to demonstrate the depth of isolation that many bereaved parents experience, how misunderstood they can feel. Again, this is where the PCA can be invaluable; the offering of deep empathy that conveys to the parent 'I'm here to really listen, to hear you and your experiences from your point of view, this is a space to talk about whatever you need to in whatever way you need, and I endeavour to the best of my abilities to understand what you are telling me'. It tells them they are not alone.

Judgement and Taboos

Judgement is something that comes up frequently in my work with bereaved parents, in all sorts of ways. I see it woven through parent's experiences;

judging themselves but also sensing it from others, wondering what people think about them, wondering if people see their grief as valid. Parents can experience judgement about the way they feel and express their grief, with feelings such as envy, unfairness, resentment and anger considered taboo to talk openly about. Bereaved parents are frequently triggered by being around pregnancy or babies and often rely on avoidance for some time after their loss. This too can be frowned upon; 'you ought to go and see the baby, you can't just avoid seeing your sister because she is pregnant, why don't you want to see the scan photos?'. I hear from parents how the type of loss can in itself lead to judgement. A SUDI death with standard procedure police involvement might lead to speculation, judgement, gossip and grief put on hold until there is some clarity about the cause of the baby's death. The heartbreaking decision for a TFMR can lead to fears of judgement from other people about the decision, complex feelings of conflict and doubts about their right to grieve as they 'made this choice'.

Many of these kinds of things go unspoken; the judgement is often implied or suggested rather than explicit, the fears of the bereaved parent are carried silently, the 'taboo' feelings they experience not talked about. It's a sort of awkward silence, where everyone is left guessing what everyone else is thinking. Here the PCA can create a safe space where these things can be discussed openly. By showing up consistently as congruent, empathic and non-judgmental with the bereaved parent, we can build a deep trust and sense of psychological safety where they can say the unsayable, and finally these feelings, experiences and worries can be brought forth into spoken acknowledgment, without judgement, a gentle noticing. The sense of relief from parents is often palpable when they realise they are not going to be judged for what happened to them or for feelings they are having. I am also often asked 'is this normal?' to which I can invariably answer honestly 'I have heard this kind of feeling or experience many times from other bereaved parents' – again the sense of relief here is readily apparent.

People Wanting to 'Fix' Things

The thing about baby loss is we can't 'fix' it; we can't bring the baby back, we can't make the grief go away. But it is a common experience of bereaved parents that some people will try nonetheless. Often this desire to 'fix' comes from a place of love and care, a desperate wish to be able to make it all better for the bereaved parent, but sometimes it comes from a place of impatience, 'why aren't you getting better by now?'. It can be difficult for the 'fixer', who might feel inadequate, confused or frustrated, as well as for the bereaved parent. The pressure, expectation, maybe even the implication that they could 'get better' if only they would do the things other people suggest can lead to parents hiding the extent of their grief, resulting in deeper isolation. Whatever the intention behind wanting to 'fix it', it is wildly missing the point.

Almost without exception, bereaved parents will tell me that you don't 'get over' the death of your baby, but rather you learn to 'live with' the loss and the grief. They tell me 'it doesn't get better, it gets different', they experience their grief as something that evolves and changes over time but it doesn't go away; they learn to carry it. For me, working with baby loss has been key in cementing my awareness that we, as person-centred counsellors, are not here to 'fix'. And when we realise this, I have found, it really frees us to fully embrace the real value of the PCA which is in how it allows us to be alongside the bereaved parent in their grief. The non-expert stance, the non-directive attitude of the PCA has given me a way to really follow the person, to listen and really hear the person in front of me, allow them to tell me their unique story, and stay with them as they begin to process their grief in their own way.

In Conclusion

A key quality that drew me to the PCA in the first place and that I am continually astounded by is its straightforwardness, the apparent simplicity of the approach; it does not strive to over-complicate matters. I don't mean by this that the PCA is superficial, or that it is 'therapy-lite' as it is sometimes mischaracterised. Quite the opposite in fact; the restrained elegance of Rogers' theories belies the great depth, connectedness, compassion and powerful therapeutic value of the PCA. It is an approach that can, at times, require great patience, enough conviction to go against the grain and the courage to 'trust the process': to have faith that, given the right conditions, and given time, the client we sit with will find a way towards growthful and therapeutic change. When we can find the wherewithal to do this, however, the value can be immense.

By its very nature, I cannot quantify the 'efficacy' of the PCA to baby loss in terms of outcomes; I strive to carry no expectation or agenda as to an 'outcome' for the parents I work with. But what I do know is what bereaved parents tell me, which is, to my mind, the most valuable and relevant measure of any therapeutic relationship. What they tell me is that this space, the person-centred counselling space, is often one of the few, or perhaps the only space where they feel really heard and understood, where they know there will be no judgement, where they don't have to worry about how their attempts to share their experiences will be met. It is a place of safety where they can dare to say the things they are thinking and feeling, where they know they will be accepted and valued regardless of what these are. It is a space where they feel no pressure or expectation about how to grieve or feel, what to think or say.

It is also, vitally, a space where they can talk freely about their beloved baby, to share the love, grief, pride, sadness, joy, longing; the whole gamut of feelings, even when they are complicated, conflicted, confusing. When trying to capture and articulate what it is we can offer when we take a person-centred approach, I often turn to a phrase of Jan Hawkins.[1] We cannot fix what has happened, but we can choose to be a 'fearless companion' alongside the bereaved parent, remaining gently, patiently, steadfastly with them as they begin to find a way to process their experiences and gradually learn to live with their profound grief and sense of loss.

Note

1 Hawkins, J., *Trauma, Dissociation and the Person-Centred Approach*. https://onlinevents.co.uk/courses/trauma-dissociation-and-the-person-centred-approach-workshop-with-jan-hawkins/

Afterword

We hope that these stories of person-centred practice from across the globe have shown that the person-centred approach (PCA) has an important role to play in responding to contemporary challenges. Through their reflection on the application of the PCA in differing but equally testing settings, these experienced person-centred and experiential practitioners have demonstrated the value of the approach and identified learning from its non-directive nature. They have debunked the myth about the PCA being 'passive' and demonstrated its merit in individual, societal and global crises. These authors work in a wide range of difficult and challenging settings, but despite their different clients, settings, issues, cultures and countries, all were offering Rogers' six necessary and sufficient conditions, and some common themes were evident in their accounts of person-centred practice.

The PCA Remains a Powerful, Transformative Approach

The person-centred approach continues to be practiced fully in the United Kingdom, Europe, New Zealand and across the globe, upholding the sustaining theory of Carl Rogers, and the central premise of his work, first stated more than 70 years ago, remains radical and effective. All the authors powerfully articulate how the application of the PCA is valuable in the challenging issues they engage with. Indeed, they show that the PCA remains relevant and has an important role to play in responding to global emergencies, international conflict, social and personal crises. Furthermore, they have shown that the approach is clearly applicable in working with trauma.

Whether in a time of war, working with unaccompanied migrant children, sitting with those experiencing profound loss or navigating trauma, we've seen that through encounters and being in relation with others, the PCA enables transformation and growth – growth in individuals, couples and organisations; growth inside the therapy room or in education, health, social care or other organisations.

Non-Directivity Is a Positive Force for Change

The concept of non-directivity emerges in all the authors' reflections on practice. Part of the inspiration for this book came from encountering scepticism about the value of 'non-direction' while working in health settings at operational and strategic levels, and as a person-centred practitioner. This is perhaps understandable in a world where it sometimes feels like everything is directed, either by tradition, habit or repute.

However, these authors repeatedly talk about their understanding and valuing of the concept of non-directivity. Even in scenarios where it would be tempting to direct the client, to develop solutions or to seek easy answers, again and again they articulate how non-directivity underpins everything in their work. Jen Keppie, in her chapter on baby loss, exemplifies this in her description of non-directivity as holding 'a deep respect for the personhood of the other'. Jen eloquently articulates how her growth in understanding non-directivity in practice has also enhanced her sense of congruence 'each supporting the other'. Similarly Jacquelyn, in her work with couples, describes with insight how offering both partners the opportunity to explore their experience of their relationship with her in a non-judgemental, validating, empathic way allows them, not her, to provide direction.

The 'Self' Is Instrumental in Effecting Change

Rogers contends that the use of self and the sharing of power between therapist and client are instrumental in effecting change. We see this throughout these stories of person-centred practice. Kate and Terry put use of self at the centre of their training programme with social care workers, enabling these carers to enhance their own self-awareness and self-acceptance. This directly impacted what they were able to bring to the caring relationship and how they could then make use of self in caring for others.

In her work with end-of-life care, Stephanie articulates how compassionately examining one's own history and being open to others' different experiences and perspectives can foster meaningful and useful discourse. She describes her embracing of the PCA as expanding her perspective and strengthening her sense of self, a sense that she then uses to respect and respond to what arises in her work. Similarly, in Chapter 6, Sonny writes of exploring their own experience of neurodivergence and then directly relating that to applying the PCA. Sonny describes the power of a person continually choosing to actively connect at a deep level with another person and the subsequent learning for person-centred practitioners.

Offering the Necessary and Sufficient Conditions Is Transformative

There is a large bank of detailed work from Rogers, and other influential thinkers who followed him, in articulating the enormity of the reach of the principles of an approach which values the other, values difference and is unconditional in relationship to the other. He was a pioneer of his time in psychology, psychotherapy and other helping professions touched on in this book. His six necessary and sufficient conditions emerged strongly in all these accounts of practice as vital to allowing individuals the freedom to grow and develop into themselves.

Perhaps Elektra in her work with ex-convicts illustrates this most succinctly in her description of how she continued to work in challenging external and societal circumstances that threatened to limit her work by being congruent, as she says 'I confronted the social realities in the same way as I encounter a client: in the here and now, with the therapeutic conditions and my authentic self as my only tools'. She and Alex, in Chapter 2, further emphasise how congruence in person-centred therapy fosters a deep connection between therapist and client. They describe how they create a safe, empathic environment, grounded in unconditional positive regard, to provide clients with a non-judgmental space where they can express their vulnerabilities and process their deep emotional experiences.

The power of being genuinely heard is deeply meaningful in human development and growth. Being valued for who you are regardless of age, colour, race, gender, disability, sexuality or politics is a way of connecting meaningfully to another human being that allows them to be seen and valued for who they are in the world. These stories illustrate how empathic communication, congruence and unconditional acceptance of others can be transformative in even the most complex, challenging situations.

You Cannot Care for Others Unless You Can Care for Yourself

While the power and effectiveness of the PCA are clear to see, one issue that emerges from these accounts of practice is the importance of self-care. These stories identified a number of barriers that arise when those from a relational and non-directive approach are engaged in complex, demanding scenarios within national and international organisations; these included burnout, workload and bureaucracy. Alex and Elektra found this in their work with migrants and asylum seekers, using this experience to develop resources to enhance emotional resilience and help sustain compassionate care. Equally, Susanna stresses the importance of keeping in contact with the person-centred and experiential community in order to feel supported in this way of being and thinking, and Mairi and Terry have shown how the core conditions along with non-directivity can provide a safe, nourishing space that allows therapists working under the most challenging of conditions to continue to support their clients.

In an age when we see services in local communities and public sector organisations being increasingly driven by nationally set budgets and targets, the need for self-care is evident. Gareth sets us some challenging questions to ponder over the potential role of AI in helping to meet and manage increasing demands. But, while AI may seem an uncomfortable idea for relational therapists, other organisational responses, such as short-term counselling, may be equally challenging and discomforting. What is clear though is the value of an ongoing commitment to supervision and the personal development of practitioners, in both preventing burnout and enhancing and sustaining the growth of the counsellor.

The Person-Centred Approach: Into the Future

We have seen how, when committing to the client in deeply respectful ways, the person-centred and experiential community is able to offer individuals the freedom to grow and develop into themselves; to become 'fully functioning persons'. We've seen the power and effectiveness of the approach and its relevance to the conflicts, crises and challenges that counsellors wrestle with today but that doesn't mean that the PCA is complacent. There is still curiosity, exploration and development of person-centred theory to try to understand the process more fully.

There are practitioners like Gareth, Sonny, Kate and Terry who are pushing into new fields and new settings; counsellors like Mairi, Jacquelyn, Elektra, Jen and Alex who don't accept that the PCA is passive and take it into scenarios that challenge and unsettle us; and those like Susanna and Stephanie, indeed all the authors, who see a greater role for the PCA than simply in the therapy room. Their innovative and inspiring practice is proposed as blueprints for future development and models of good practice for all person-centred and experiential practitioners.

Index

FSC
www.fsc.org
MIX
Papier | Fördert gute Waldnutzung
FSC® C083411

Kolibri 360 GmbH
Ferdinand-Jühlke-Straße 7
99095 Erfurt, Deutschland
produktsicherheit@kolibri360.de